FILM RESEARCH

A Critical Bibliography

with

Annotations and Essay

Compiled by

Peter J. Bukalski

G. K. HALL & CO., 70 LINCOLN STREET, BOSTON, MASS.

1972

Library of Congress Cataloging in Publication Data

Bukalski, Peter J
  Film research.

  1. Moving-pictures--Bibliography. I. Title.
Z5784.M9B897   016.79143   72-3794
ISBN 0-8161-0971-0

This publication is printed on permanent/durable acid-free paper.

© Peter J. Bukalski 1972

Ref
Z
5784
.M9
B897

ISBN 0-8161-0971-0

TABLE OF CONTENTS

I. Film Research .... page 1

II. Essential Works .... page 28

III. Film Rental .... page 39

IV. Film Purchase .... page 47

V. Film Periodicals .... page 51

VI. Using the Bibliography .... page 66

VII. The Major Bibliography .... page 70

    Category 1: Film History, Theory, Criticism and Introductory Works .... page 71

    Category 2: Film Production and Technology 1 -- Contemporary .... page 98

    Category 3: Film Production and Technology 2 -- Of Historical Interest .... page 110

    Category 4: Film Genre .... page 117

    Category 5: Sociology and Economics of Film .... page 122

    Category 6: National Cinemas .... page 130

    Category 7: Film Scripts .... page 136

    Category 8: Particular Films .... page 144

    Category 9: Personalities, Biographies, and Filmographies .... page 149

    Category 10: Film Education .... page 180

    Category 11: Film-Related Works .... page 190

    Category 12: Careers in Film .... page 193

    Category 13: Bibliographies, Guides, and Indexes ... page 195

    Category 14: Selected Works in Foreign Languages ... page 202

FILM RESEARCH

If current publication rates are any indication of the developing status of a discipline, film is certainly one of the fastest growing new fields of research and inquiry. There is no parallel to the tremendous growth of serious interest in film which has occurred in the last fifteen years. The number of serious scholars working in the field of film has never been greater. In the last five years the growth of cinema literature has been truly phenominal, with new volumes appearing at an unprecedented rate. This growth is in part due to the efforts of the ever-increasing ranks of cinema writers, researchers, and critics, and in part due to the seemingly insatiable appetite of the reading public for film books. Obviously not all of the new cinema literature is of great value, but in whatever area an interest exists a volume soon appears. Everywhere, it seems, serious intellectual interest in film is growing at an unprecedented rate. In the academic sphere film has begun to be recognized as a distinct new discipline, due to the tremendous growth of film courses in the colleges and universities of America. Whereas ten years ago there were only a handful of institutions which offered courses in film, today there are hundreds. The American Film Institute's Guide to College Film Courses seems to quadruple in size each year. And largely because of the leadership of many fine educators film has begun to make an impact on other levels of American education: film study courses are becoming increasingly common in high schools and film making has even been integrated into the curriculum of lower and middle schools.

The complex and exciting art film climate of the sixties is partially credited with awakening interest in film. Observing the current scene, many mistakenly felt that film had suddenly become an art form after existing for decades as a "mere entertainment" medium. But research revealed to the less informed what had always been apparent to older scholars--that film had long been a complex and dynamic art form. The vast viewing public, often unfamiliar with the great European and American film masterpieces, somehow imagined that film had evolved into a true art form in the course of a single decade. What formerly seemed unworthy of comment suddenly became the most talked-about and controversial fine art. As the decade of the sixties ended and the seventies began, interest in film went on growing at ever higher rates and the explosion of knowledge about film continued unabated.

Film, as a result of this recent explosion of writing and research, is now in its early stages of development as an academic discipline. And, like other incompletely defined disciplines, it has yet to develop a cohesive, unifying philosophy of study. Since film has not long existed as an academic field almost all writers, researchers, and commentators bring to film a background in another, older discipline. Writers, researchers, and scholars often strive to understand film with the mental structures which their previous training has given them, not realizing the prejudices which their fields and the operational procedures of those fields have imposed on them. **Training in** any other academic discipline carries with it, however subtlely, attitudes, methodology, and a perceptual apparatus which may be too narrow, too incomplete, or simply insufficiently applicable to the field of film. The unfortunate results of attempts to apply the disciplinary methods of other fields to the motion picture are daily evident--volumes which, however well intended, fail to capture anything that is truly "cinematic."

It is unfortunate that many young scholars, frustrated in their own overcrowded fields, have gravitated quite unprepared to film in hopes of achieving instant status and recognition. The volumes resulting from their vehement but often fruitless conflicts with one another make very dull reading indeed.

With the multiplicity of viewpoints which are ever operative in the film field, it seems imperative that the film researcher be able to successfully evaluate the validity of each author's approach, so that his own viewpoint will be unfettered and objective. And while many works claim to have authoritative answers to all cinematic questions, it must be remembered that the field as a whole has yet to develop even a few major schools of thought. It also seems imperative that the film writer/researcher be aware of the many basic analytical assumptions of film writers. While many of the current writers are versed in only narrow aspects of film, due in part to their previous academic training, it is hoped that a new generation will arise which will produce the truly authoritative film works.

Point of view, then, is one of the greatest problems of film research today. The problem of point of view is crucial to the further development of film. It would appear unlikely that human knowledge can be significantly advanced by individuals attempting to apply perceptual tools and academic methodologies only slightly adapted from the disciplines to which they are organic. Rather, progress will be made when a disciplinary view is established which is essentially and completely filmic. It is likely that the current generation will see this evolution of the film field occur. In the meantime it is enormously important for the researcher to be aware of the viewpoints at work today, in order to evaluate the validity of each work and to avoid each work's limitations.

Many writers and scholars attempt to take an overly literary approach to film. This approach has in part been popularized by the large number of individuals now in the film field whose primary training was in English literature. Despite the insights which a literary analysis can sometimes provide, few writers using this approach can successfully deal with a motion picture as a total entity. Too often film technique is simply viewed as an alternate means of projecting the verbal meanings of a printed page: technique as an element of film form is largely neglected. The influence of film technique and, particularly, acting on an audience's perception of a film is not understood. Obviously, with this literary orientation the importance of the fiction film is emphasized to the detriment of other film genre. Moreover, the greatest difficulty inherent in an approach oriented toward literature is that it works best with the film script rather than with the film itself. Literary analysis presumes the opportunity to stop, review, and search for meanings with complete flexibility. However, film is a temporal art and as such it must make its real impact in a limited period of time. Thus the literary approach totally neglects the experiential aspects of film. And as the range of film increases such a limited approach seems less and less appropriate for the increasingly abstract and nonverbal films of today.

While a literary orientation overemphasizes the importance of the fictional motion picture, undue concern for film solely as a form of communication can artificially inflate the importance of the documentary and informational film. And although communication specialists have provided valuable insights into the nature of film perception, one must constantly remind oneself when reading works with a communication orientation that the artistic aspects of film are at least as important as its communicative aspects.

In earlier times, when films (at least American films) seemed more standardized than they do now, a dramatic or theatrical approach to film was often quite workable. "Theatrical" critics were often concerned with the group aspects of film production: it was important to them to differentiate and identify the contribution of each of the many artists in the film production chain. Dramatic theory provided a valuable tool for analyzing film structure. Acting, the chief expressive tool of the legitimate theatre, was also given considerable attention. This point of view was valuable for long periods of American film history when the contributions of photography, editing, and sound seemed to be of lesser importance. But, as the range of film increased, dramatic theory could not offer insights into many complex nonlinear films. And acting increasingly has been deemphasized as a means of filmic expression.

A modern viewpoint which is still quite popular, despite its seemingly obvious shortcomings, is the use of "auteur" theory to seek insights into the nature of film. Popularized by the French, auteur theory views each film as the product of its director--his attitudes, his prejudices, his artistic taste. The director is viewed as the "author" or "architect" of the completed film. This critical attitude had great application to the dominant French directors of the fifties and sixties and to other highly individual directors. However, this doctrine obviously was later overapplied. Until recent years few directors in America had a significant influence on the scripts they produced. The auteur theory very obviously neglects the group aspect of film production, which is so important to theatrically-oriented critics. Most importantly, in this theory the film writer is completely deemphasized as a significant figure in the movie making process. Thus, like so many points of view, this one has proved inadequate since it evaluates films against an abstract theoretical standard rather than attempting to understand the film as an entity in itself.

Virtually all writing about motion pictures takes as truth an aesthetic question which has been debated for centuries. All motion picture writing <u>assumes</u> the relevance of the form-content distinction, and writers, by their very incognizance, accept this basic aesthetic consideration. The acceptance of the form-content distinction has a long historical precedent in film. In the earliest films, such as those of the Lumière brothers in France and of Edison in America, spectators view a real event to which the camera was <u>added</u> for recording purposes. Later, when the film had progressed beyond the recording of actuality to the fiction film (as with the Film d'Art), a stage play served as subject with a camera <u>added</u> simply as a recording device. Thus the action (later the "content") was always distinctly separate from the recorder, the camera. It was as if the two occupied different spheres between which there lay an impenetrable gulf. The film then unwittingly assumed a nineteenth-century theatrical principle-- the separation into separate entities of the action (play) and observer (audience-camera). Even when film abandoned the technique of the static camera (the view of the ideal spectator), the theatrical principle continued to prevail, since scenes were staged <u>for</u> the camera (to obtain the best view), this accepting the idea that the camera was a foreign object introduced into--but always separate from--the scene. As film technique developed and was recognized, writers continued to make the mental separation of the content of the film from the manner in which it was produced. Thus, while aesthetic consideration of the relationship between film form and film content continued, the door had been opened for the development of film philosophies which emphasized one concept at the expense of the other.

So it is that we find writers who specialize in one or another aspect of the total film art form. Within the content sphere of the work of art, some commentators dwell on the "meaning" of the film, oblivious to the fact that this is an arbitrary dissection of the total work of art. Others search for the "truth" of the human condition in film, judging a motion picture on the basis of its insights into the "reality" of life. An inappropriate standard is applied because, obviously, not all films make an attempt in this direction. Still other writers take great delight in the structural aspects of content, enthusiastically pointing out each new method of arranging a series of events. As a typical example of overemphasis on content, a number of recent books have explored religious values in commercial motion pictures. Writers, while discovering interesting ethical and moral parallels, have often failed to realize that mere complexity does not make a good film. A film's religious overtones might make an interesting study, but these insights may not give the spectator much of an understanding of the film as a whole. Nor would such overtones make a film a significant one.

It is unfortunate that many writers confuse the reality of a film with what they perceive as the reality of life. A comparison of the events of a film with the reality from which they were drawn can produce some valuable insights. However, this is obviously an incomplete view of the totality of a film. A film, like any other work of art, can create its own sense of "reality." In this regard I can recall one writer who criticized the film Bonnie and Clyde because it did not give a truthful picture of the real-life characters on whom it was based. The relationship of the reality of film to the reality of life as perceived by the critic was at question. Too often commentators condemn a film because its reality does not conform to their experience. We must remember that film as an art form cannot be expected constantly to reflect "truth" as interpreted by the viewer.

If there have been excesses in the analysis of the content sphere of film art, there have been greater ones in the form sphere. Here many young researchers, in well-motivated but premature attempts, have glorified each unusual camera angle, each bizarrely illogical sound. But, obviously, experimental technique does not necessarily make a contribution to the impact of the film. Much of the overemphasis on film technique is seen in the work of writers new to the field, to whom the whole subject seems an eye-opening revelation. Many new writers, following admirable self-education programs, have overreacted to their discoveries. Film theorists have had an important influence here also. Until recently very little film theory found its way into print, and that which did was often extreme in its viewpoint. While mature scholars have long since placed the major film theories in perspective, many younger writers have yet to understand them adequately. Typical of the overemphasis on film technique has been the recent rage among novices for Orson Welles' first film, Citizen Kane. Arthur Knight in his very fine book, The Liveliest Art, properly assesses Citizen Kane, finding it inferior to the later, more mature Magnificent Ambersons. Welles' flamboyant and showy film technique appeals to many film writers, at least partially because it can so easily be admired, and they fail to realize, as Knight does, that <u>Citizen Kane as a whole</u> is more impressive than moving.

Often critics and aestheticians in film, as in other fields, seem unable to integrate perceptions and emotional responses to art on the one hand with purely aesthetic or formal analysis on the other. Of the two, the second can more easily be dealt with and broken down into principles. Perceptions are at best elusive, and emotional responses can seldom be measured or adequately described. Therefore, philosophies of formal analysis of works of art have much appeal. It would appear, however, that film more than any of the other arts cannot be adequately explained without using both approaches. While it is evident that the <u>experience</u> of film viewing is what appeals to the vast movie-going public, it is also true that film has many highly complex formal aspects, some derived from the theatre, some from its status as a visual art.

Defending formalist writers for a moment, one must admit some artistic appreciation of film is contemplation of spatial, plastic, temporal, and color relationships. (Why else would purely abstract animations and psychedelic films have such appeal?) Such contemplation of artistic form is often described as being divorced of all presuppositions and associations of the spectator. Increasingly, many critics insist that form is the only proper subject for film analysis: but even the late critic and formalist aesthetician Roger Fry admitted that purely formal contemplation of a work of art is actually quite rare and more commonly blends with content-contemplation in which past associations do play a part.

Here we come to an interesting point: film is the rorschach of the fine arts. More than any other art, film seems to elicit responses which are often more revealing of the commentator than of the film. As films became increasingly ambiguous in the current decade, critics increasingly found contradictory meanings in the same film. Past associations play such an enormous part in the response of any film viewer that one wonders if any degree of critical objectivity is possible. Obviously, a purely formal approach to film would appear to be highly impossible.

The problem of analysis is additionally complicated by the fact that film form presents a more difficult analytical problem than that encountered in the other arts. The arrangement of subject matter or events (plot/film structure) of the motion picture, largely communicated verbally, has frequently been the subject of formal analysis. At the same time, single pictures or frames from movies have been analyzed much as a painting would be examined. Thus, film form is dual: it exists on both visual and audible levels. Recent writers who have attempted new, more organic descriptions of film form have sometimes discussed it as "images" and "sounds." While this is a new arrangement in some respects, the duality of film form remains an intact concept.

It must also be pointed out that purely formal appreciation of art is a cultivated response since it attempts to divorce the normal one-within-another relationship which exists between form and content. Purely formal appreciation of film is difficult since the motion picture shares with the theatre a physiologically and psychologically based factor of empathy. The special type of empathy (as distinct from that which is part of appreciation of the theatre) which the film viewer enjoys has long been one of the major appeals of the motion picture. Unfortunately, empathy has never been adequately defined and studies explicating its effect still await the design of adequate experimental methodology.

There clearly remains a great deal regarding the "meaning" of a work of art which purely formal analysis will not reveal. New levels of insight can be reached through the explication of the social, political, economic, philosophical and cultural traditions of any film, its artists, and the country which produced it. Content analysis, it seems to me, is essential to reaching adequate understanding of an art form as complex as film.

The distinction between form and content must inevitably blur since form can be the carrier of content conveyed in the form of a convention. In the visual arts, religious painting frequently uses conventions to project a complexity of meanings. The plotting of American westerns can be said to be a formal design element which carries with it a mass of associations and meanings.

With the rush of many young writers into form analysis, it would appear inevitable that the experiential aspects of film would frequently be downgraded or ignored. True, it is more difficult to speak articulately about the emotional and sensual aspect of any artistic experience: yet for many individuals the experience of film viewing is the most profound reaction to art they will ever know. Despite this, many writers reject experiential aspects of art as being somehow beneath consideration, as if any noncerebral activity is unworthy of a true scholar. Nonetheless, many films obviously seek to evoke emotional responses. Film is not a private art, but is intended for group viewing with empathic participation: to ignore this aspect would appear to preclude any true understanding of the nature of film art.

The conflict that seems to exist between the philosophies of purely formal analysis on the one hand and purely content analysis on the other appears to be detrimental to the further development of film knowledge. More than any other art form, film clearly and probably requires a flexible approach. Some films must be discussed almost solely in terms of content (since their formal aspects are so standard and undistinguished) while other films, devoid of normal subject matter, can only be understood and appreciated in formal terms. Most films require a balanced approach for adequate comprehension and appreciation. The complexity of film technique, involving as it does a multitude of twentieth-century inventions, and the universality of film content, cry out for a complete yet flexible analytical philosophy.

In summation, the problem existent is that too many motion picture researchers attempt to write from a theoretical viewpoint which is too narrow and individual. Such a viewpoint by <u>its very definition</u> excludes whole portions of the realm of the motion picture.

In the past two decades a large number of volumes have been published which are little more than elaborate (and often quite emotional) justifications for a particular film viewpoint. The first half of one recent book, for instance, is almost entirely devoted to denunciations of other recent books. Certainly this is not productive. The very emotion with which so many new film works are written is an indication of the strong conflicts which are developing in the field. It seems unfortunate that so many writers spend a lifetime defending a viewpoint which probably was too hastily conceived in the first place. I am not denying that most film books are of some value. Rather, I will argue that most film researchers/writers have yet to develop a film philosophy which is sufficiently eclectic to embrace <u>all</u> film. It is impossible to deny that this is an ideal, that each writer as an individual is bound to have his particular prejudices. However, film research has not kept pace with the widening range of film since World War II: instead of greater sophistication on the part of writers we have many attempts to justify narrow, specialized philosophies. As the range of the film increases, so does the need for the critic/scholar who can foster appreciation through explications of historical, cultural, social, and technical film traditions. Many viewpoints might be partially valid, but not all can be applied equally to all types of films. The goal of new entrants into the field should be to engage in ever wider, ever more knowledgeable, and ever more generic studies of film.

The education of film writers and researchers in the history and development of the art has increasingly become a matter of concern. Lack of familiarity with the great works of British and American literature would be unthinkable for a literary critic, yet most film commentators have never seen the great masterpieces in the history of film. More ridiculously, writers have frequently dismissed historical films as mere primitive art. An attitude of historical appreciation is sometimes missing even among cinema historians (as evidenced by Kenneth Macgowan's Behind the Screen). Clearly, historical motion picture appreciation is in its infant stages in this country and is awaiting further development along the path charted by art historians.

What passes for film history is often merely gossip or ridiculous annecdotes. Descriptions of films often attempt to explain them away rather than offer significant insights. Little has been written attempting to reconstruct initial audience reaction to an historic film, and even less has been discovered to elucidate modern audience reaction.

Adequate appreciation of historical films should involve an in-depth understanding of now obsolete motion picture technology. Little effort has been made to recreate the original "look" of early motion pictures, a common preoccupation in other art forms. It is obvious that little real historical research has actually been carried out in the motion picture field: the surface has barely been scratched.

Recently an increasing number of works have attempted to define the distinct nature of film as a total art form. These searches for the "purely cinematic" or the "language of film" are of immense value since they strive to define a complete aesthetic of film. Most of these studies focus on one or both of two concepts--the characteristics of the motion picture (i.e., medium) and individual treatment of these characteristics (style).

Since each film artist must work within the limitations and potentials of his medium, it stands to reason that a complete exploration of the possibilities of the medium will provide some insights into the quality and imagination of the work of art. Most theorists exploring an art form try to reach an understanding of it through an examination of known examples. And while most art forms have existed for centuries, making a wide range of works (exemplifying the possibilities of the medium) available for study, film is a young art. Thus, a discussion of its possibilities only in terms of known examples is bound to become rapidly dated as artists find new means of using the medium expressively. Two good examples of excellent works which became dated are Rudolph Arnheim's <u>Film as Art</u> and Raymond Spottiswoode's <u>A Grammar of the Film</u>. Both of these works, originally published in the early part of the sound era, provided valuable and detailed explications of silent film aesthetics. Their consideration of sound film proved inadequate simply because examples at the time were not really representative of the potential of sound.

In comparison with the other arts film has many possibilities which remain unexplored. Moreover, developing technology constantly increases the potential of the medium, adding to the unexplored possibilities. In attempting to fill in the gaps between known examples and thus extend the lives of their books, many writers have predicted future developments of the film medium. Most of these attempts seem silly or incomplete in retrospect, although a few have proved devastatingly accurate. New and exciting developments of the medium all too often quickly drop from view, sometimes because of overuse and other times because of insufficient critical and public interest.

There is a danger in becoming too preoccupied with medium characteristics. If the great artist by definition takes delight in the skilled manipulation of his medium, it is easily possible to misinterpret technical and formal experiments for true masterpieces of art. Likewise, it is ridiculous to downgrade a work of art simply because it fails to extend the reaches of the art form. Is it not possible to employ the medium uniquely in a work which is unsatisfactory as a whole? Many film writers of late have increasingly mistaken innovation for true creativity and showmanship for artistry. To the true scholar, understanding of the medium is only one means of finding insights into the elusive nature of film.

If the description of existing film works in the aforegoing text has often seemed negative, it is an indication of the amount of meaningful research which remains to be done. As in many new fields, opportunities abound in film for an individual to produce original, significant, and even pioneering research. There are many film subjects about which only a few books of any value have been written. There are areas in which virtually nothing at all has been published. And as the current rash of publications indicates, interest in all film subjects runs high. It would be impossible to enumerate all the areas deserving attention: however, a few are discussed below.

While many works dealing with film history are in wide circulation, only a few can be said to be of value. Many early histories consisted of material which was little different from that of popular film magazines. In contrast, Kevin Brownlow's <u>The Parade's Gone by</u> was widely heralded a few years ago, largely because it drew heavily from actual interviews with many of the remaining film personnel of the silent era rather than from inexpert suppositions. Some so-called film history has been too preoccupied with the careers of various stars or with the political maneuvers within Hollywood studios. Books offering an in-depth study of selected areas of film history are much in demand. More importantly, works which foster <u>historical appreciation</u> are much needed. There is a special need to reconstruct the original condition of many films. For instance, no one is really certain if many classic films which today are available for viewing are still edited in their original order. Attempts to restore the original condition of historical films are extremely rare. It is frequently forgotten that silent films were never really silent, but were always accompanied by some type of musical score. Few of these scores have been authoritatively reconstructed. The aesthetic effect of these scores remains largely undetermined. Before the perfection of color photography, film was often chemically tinted to follow the moods of the motion picture. This effect has seldom been accurately reconstructed. Modern critics need to be able to experience classic films in their original form. Most importantly, the great film masterpieces of the past must be understood within the context of the socio-cultural conditions which produced them. Little has been written about this aspect of early classic films. Clearly, film history is in its infant stages of development, with little actual research taking place. There is a great need for extensive research to fill in the gaps in our historical knowledge.

Just as historical appreciation remains to be adequately developed, a multitude of aspects of the contemporary film remain to be thoroughly explored. The individual has never before been faced with such a bewildering variety of films, all of which he is expected to comprehend and appreciate. And while many highly individualistic film stylists (Antonioni, Bergman, Fellini) have been given considerable attention, little has been written to explicate the effects of social and cultural traditions of the producing countries on recent films. Unfortunately, most commentators seem to feel that expressing their own personal reactions to a film is all that is required of them, as if any valid artistic judgment could be made in complete ignorance and isolation. While film research becomes increasingly complex each year, we have a long way to go to match the sophistication of researchers and critics in other fine arts fields. Film has not yet produced a man of the stature of Erwin Panofsky: writers with his knowledge and insights are sorely needed in the field of motion pictures.

Despite the number of new works which purport to examine the essential nature of film as an art form, much remains to be done in this area. Of these many new works, few have been widely accepted by persons in the field. There certainly has been far too much emphasis placed on proselytizing and too little attention paid to dispassionate scholarship.

Of tremendous interest today is the interplay between society and the art of film. While many studies have attempted to prove that film has had a profound influence on society and its values, and on the individual's psychology, these studies have often been inconclusive. Studies designed to prove that film has only reflected the values of society have been equally inconclusive. Most "scientific" studies of film are simply too narrow in scope to offer any extensive insights into the nature of film. A number of recent works examine the sociology of film, but are simply not broad or complete enough to be considered authoritative. The reasons for the popular appeal of some motion pictures have not been significantly examined. And while some scholars feel such studies would be of little significance, they certainly could prove enlightening.

The experience of film viewing remains a largely unexplored topic. The influence of audience situations on individual perception awaits study, as do the factors which appear to make each viewing of a film a different experience. The entire emotion-evoking mechanism of filmic perception has not been thoroughly explored.

The potential researcher must remember that in most areas of film research it is the motion picture itself which is the primary source. No amount of related printed material can substitute for the viewing of a motion picture. Access to particular film titles has long been the greatest difficulty facing any serious scholar. If one were fortunate to live in New York or Los Angeles a glimpse of selected films could be obtained at archives, in private collections, or in commercial revivals. But even there access has been erratic, and certainly the scholar's need for particular titles has gone unheeded. The lack of adequate access to the bulk of world film production is no doubt responsible for the inadequacy of many scholarly works. One can only guess how many film historians have eloquently tried to describe a film which they themselves have distantly remembered.

The status of accessibility to titles has improved, but only slightly. It is now possible to rent for private viewing many motion pictures which were formerly confined to archives. The outright purchase of films increasingly presents an attractive alternative to the scholar/researcher, although the current list of available titles is not extensive. Fortunately, ever greater numbers of libraries and information centers are recognizing the need of scholars and students for films and are attempting to meet this need.

When the American Film Institute was founded it pledged to develop archives to preserve the American film heritage. This effort was painfully long overdue, since many American films had long since disappeared and others, stored and forgotten, had deteriorated so badly that they were about to disintegrate completely. The Institute also pledged to develop film research facilities and, in particular, to work to increase the availability of films so that virtually any needed title could be made available to scholars everywhere in the United States. The American Film Institute began its work with a considerable time disadvantage over similar institutes in France, Great Britain, Denmark and elsewhere. Nonetheless, the Institute has been successful in locating and preserving original negatives and copies of films which long were thought lost. The extensive development of research facilities, and more importantly, the increased availability of films to scholars, remain two unaccomplished goals. Most organizations which own films feel that releasing them for scholarly study, even under very carefully controlled conditions, would somehow jeopardize chances for commercial earnings. It is hoped that the American Film Institute can obtain the cooperation of the film industry and thus provide the materials which are now so desperately needed.

There are two older American archives which are good examples of existing research facilities. The Museum of Modern Art in New York has long been active in film, maintaining an impressive archive of both films and film-related materials. The Museum has generated a number of significant publications and has an extremely impressive record in the research field. Its facilities, although in heavy use, are available to serious researchers. It is unfortunate, however, that only a portion of the films which its archives possess are now available for viewing.

The Library of Congress' Motion Picture Section has for many years maintained an enormous collection of materials. While the loan of materials is usually not possible, every attempt is made to make the collection accessible to serious scholars. Of particular interest is the paper print collection of early (and previously largely forgotten) silent films.

Existing film archives, even if duplicated in multiples, would probably not benefit the vast majority of film researchers, simply because their scattered geographic locations regrettably prohibit extensive use. Increasingly, researchers rent or buy the films which they need for intensive study. Each of these methods has its disadvantages, yet each year more material is available than ever before. Sixteen millimeter film rental agencies formerly devoted themselves primarily to popular entertainment films which appealed to schools, church groups, and clubs. With the growth of film societies interested in historical and art films, and also with the growth of film study courses in the colleges and universities of America, came the demand for an ever-widening range of film titles. It is now possible to view many significant films which have not been seen commercially for thirty years or more. But, unfortunately for the researcher/scholar, rental agencies are businesses and as such are unconcerned with the special needs of such an individual. As the list of offerings expands, however, the film rental agencies nevertheless are able to perform a valuable service to the film researcher.

Purchase increasingly is becoming a highly practical means of obtaining a film needed for prolonged examination. It is now possible to buy many of the masterpieces of the silent film era in an 8mm reduction print for fifty dollars or less. Unfortunately, the range of films available is not great. While it is possible to purchase many silent classics, fewer sound films are available. Copyrights, of course, restrict availability. Locating and obtaining consent from the owner or owners is often a problem. The economics of the film industry have often been so complex that determining the true owner of a film is often difficult. In addition, there frequently exists the more difficult problem of locating either the original negative or a print in suitable condition for copying. As is the case with film rentals, business interests reign supreme over the needs of scholarship. As long as there is money to be made in reissues and selective rentals, a film will not be released for direct sale. It is inevitable, however, that as the range of titles increases and as the prices continue to be appealing, more and more libraries and research facilities will attempt to make classic films available for their patrons.

Perhaps the ultimate in film availability will be a product of the same technological development which produced the motion picture in the first place. Recently, considerable enthusiasm has been shown for various forms of cartridged motion pictures. Janus Films, an exclusive distributor of many contemporary films, considered renting its features for long periods of time in Super 8 sound cartridges. While this idea was later rejected, the concept was exciting to scholars. The rapid development of video tape cartridges might eventually lead to the widespread availability of many films which are of interest to scholars. We must continue to hope that titles of sufficient interest will also prove to be commercially profitable.

This volume was created with the intention of providing as valuable a tool to researchers as possible, thus advancing the state of film knowledge. I hope that the various materials contained herein will be valuable both for the education of the individual and for specific research projects. In the brilliant period of discoveries foreseen ahead, I hope that Film Research will play a small but perhaps not insignificant part.

ESSENTIAL WORKS

Any essential works list is bound to be a somewhat arbitrary selection of books reflecting the personal tastes and prejudices of the author. Inevitably, difficult choices were made in selecting the fifty books which appear below. Many works of considerable merit were simply too specialized to be included. Other once valuable works have become dated and no longer seem as significant as they once did. Nonetheless, the following list will give the individual a certain minimum familiarity with the literature of the cinema.

INTRODUCTORY WORKS

Bobker, Lee R. Elements of Film. New York: Harcourt, Brace and World, 1969.

>One of the most widely read introductory works, despite its somewhat unfavorable reception by film scholars. Mr. Bobker does a reasonable job of discussing technical knowledge and

its creative application, but the extremely narrow range of examples in the book is almost embarrassing. Most importantly, a narrow and provincial attitude makes some chapters of dubious value.

Jacobs, Lewis (editor). The Emergence of the Film Art. New York: Hopkinson and Blake, 1969.

No essential works list could fail to include one of Mr. Jacob's helpful anthologies. While organized historically, The Emergence of Film Art serves as a useful introduction to many of the problems and potentials of the film field. Includes interesting material on recent developments.

Montagu, Ivor. Film World: A Guide to Cinema. Baltimore: Penguin Books, 1964.

Film World is one of the most complete yet detailed introductions to the film field. While the book is sometimes stylistically difficult, it is well worth exploring.

Talbot, Daniel (editor). Film: An Anthology. Berkeley, California: University of California Press, 1966.

This book provides valuable and informative readings on most aspects of the motion picture. While the quality of the different selections varies, many are exceptionally fine. A useful and complete introductory anthology.

FILM HISTORY

Bardèche, Maurice, and Brasillach, Robert. The History of Motion Pictures. New York: Arno Press, 1970 (reprint).

One of the early and now classic motion picture histories which is still widely read, largely for a French view of the American motion picture. Despite factual errors, well worth reading for its frequently unique viewpoint. The original 1938 edition has here been reprinted.

Brownlow, Kevin. *The Parade's Gone by*. New York: Alfred A. Knopf, 1968.

>A widely heralded history of the silent film. The author's many interviews with the directors and stars of the era are often enlightening if somewhat nostalgic. Handsomely illustrated and printed.

Ceram, C. W. (pseudonym). *Archaeology of Cinema*. New York: Harcourt, Brace and World, 1965.

>An immensely detailed account of the prehistory of the motion picture. Much attention is paid to the multitude of inventions and to nineteenth-century technology, both of which made the later emergence of the art form possible.

Crowther, Bosley. *The Lion's Share*. New York: E. P. Dutton, 1957.

>Although actually a history of MGM, *The Lion's Share* examines much that is revealing of the history of the entire industry. An extremely interesting work by the distinguished critic emeritus of *The New York Times*.

Fielding, Raymond. *A Technological History of Motion Pictures and Television*. Berkeley: University of California Press, 1967.

>Dr. Fielding's highly detailed book is the best work in one volume to examine this highly important and often neglected aspect of motion picture history.

Fulton, Albert R. *Motion Pictures: The Development of an Art from the Silent Film to the Age of Television*. Norman, Oklahoma: University of Oklahoma Press, 1960.

>A widely read film history and one which contains some interesting film analyses. Unfortunately, it suffers from an overly literary approach to the medium.

Hampton, Benjamin B. *A History of the Movies*. New York: Arno Press, 1970 (reprint).

> One of the very early and highly limited volumes of motion picture history. Hampton is valuable for his account of the growth of the industry as opposed to the art form. The original 1931 edition is here reprinted.

Knight, Arthur. The Liveliest Art. New York: Mentor Books, 1957.

> Probably the finest film history book ever written. Although admittedly a survey, it is often extremely detailed but always clear and incisive. The account of contemporary films, due to the volume's publication date, is now becoming dated. A book which one always comes back to for its frequently remarkable insights and completeness.

Macgowan, Kenneth. Behind the Screen: The History and Techniques of the Motion Picture. New York: Dell Publishing Company, 1967.

> Kenneth Macgowan was perhaps a better stylist than film scholar. His Behind the Screen is extremely interesting reading if somewhat inadequate as film history. It is best in its accounts of the technological developments of film, but less than inadequate in its discussion of many historical films. Filled with thousands of bits of useful information.

Ramsaye, Terry. A Million and One Nights: A History of the Motion Picture through 1925. New York: Simon and Schuster, 1964 (reprint).

> Although some of the factual material in this volume has been recently discredited, the work remains a lively account of the history of the early silent era. A classic work which is here reprinted from the original 1926 edition.

Rotha, Paul, and Griffith, Richard. The Film Till Now: A Survey of World Cinema. New York: Twayne Publishers, 1960.

> A critical and analytical survey of film history. The original 1930 edition is here followed by a number of sections updating the work. A classic work, best when dealing with the presound years of film history.

Vardac, A. Nicholas. Stage to Screen. New York: Benjamin Blom, 1968 (reprint).

>This scholarly and authoritative study examines the ways the nineteenth-century theatre precursed the appearance of the motion picture. The various theatrical influences on the early motion picture are examined at length. This now-classic work is here reprinted from the 1949 edition.

CONTEMPORARY FILM

Geduld, Harry M. (editor). Film Makers on Film Making. Bloomington, Indiana: Indiana University Press, 1968.

>An uneven collection of writings on film, mostly contemporary. Several highly articulate, meaningful articles.

Houston, Penelope. The Contemporary Cinema. Baltimore: Penguin Books, 1963.

>Although Penelope Houston's account leaves off in the early sixties, it is valuable for its assessment of the films of the late forties and fifties. While not totally satisfactory, the account does offer insights into many of the earlier great films of the contemporary era.

Sarris, Andrew. Interviews with Film Directors. Indianapolis: Bobbs-Merrill, 1967

>Includes interviews with a great many important contemporary film directors. Of particular value are Sarris' introductory comments and the individual filmographies.

FILM THEORY

Arnheim, Rudolph. Film as Art. Berkeley: University of California Press, 1957.

One of the classic works of film aesthetics and one which is
still imminently sensible and readable. Originally written in
the early part of the sound era, its discussion of sound has
unfortunately become dated. However, it is still a valuable
work.

Bazin, Andre. What Is Cinema? (Translated by Hugh Gray.) Berkeley: University of California Press, 1967 and 1971 (two volumes).

Bazin's classical and widely influential work was long available
only in French. Bazin's often illusive prose has been admirably translated by Dr. Gray for these editions.

Eisenstein, Sergei. Film Form and Film Sense. Cleveland: World Publishing Company, 1957.

Two classic works which are probably the most widely read
of all theoretical writings. Although often elusive,
Eisenstein's writings have proved stimulating to several generations of scholars.

Kracauer, Siegfried. Theory of Film: The Redemption of Physical Reality. New York: Oxford University Press, 1960

Although rejected by many scholars, Kracauer's theories
have nonetheless stimulated wide discussion. Although often
pretentious, his writing is shrewd and always provocative.

Lawson, John H. Film: The Creative Process. New York: Hill and Wang, 1964.

An interesting book which mainly examines the application of
Marxist theory to film. Although presented in an historical
format, its approach to history is extremely narrow.

Linden, George W. Reflections on the Screen. Belmont, California: Wadsworth Publishing Company, 1970.

Despite its enormous pretentiousness and persistently irritating semantic games, Reflections on the Screen does provide some valuable insights into the nature of film. The theoretical portions of the work are of greater value than the author's seemingly erratic examination of particular films.

Lindgren, Ernest. *The Art of the Film*. New York: The Macmillan Company, 1962 (reprint).

One of the best introductory film theory works. Written with great clarity and incisiveness, it is illustrated with excellent examples from classic films. Of enormous value.

MacCann, Richard D. (editor). *Film: A Montage of Theories*. New York: E. P. Dutton, 1966.

An excellent anthology of film theory. Includes most of the important writers and does an extremely adequate job of surveying the entire subject.

Munsterberg, Hugo. *The Photoplay, a Psychological Study*. New York: Dover Publications, 1969 (reprint).

A reprint of the original 1916 edition, this work by the eminent and prolific Hugo Munsterberg is still of great value.

Nicoll, Allardyce. *Film and Theatre*. New York: Thomas Y. Crowell, 1936.

The classic discussion of the relationship between film and theatre. Includes many valuable insights into the nature of film art.

Pudovkin, V. I. *Film Technique and Film Acting*. New York: Grove Press, 1960.

This work ranks second only to Eisenstein's as a film theory classic. Although of lesser value than the Eisenstein work, it is still basic to a comprehension of the field.

Spottiswoode, Raymond. A Grammar of the Film. Berkeley: University of California Press, 1962 (reprint).

> An early work on film aesthetics which ranks with Arnheim's Film as Art as an authoritative description of silent film aesthetics. The inadequacy of its approach to sound film is appraised in the introduction of this reprint (original date 1935).

Stephenson, Ralph, and Debrix, Jean R. The Cinema as Art. Baltimore: Penguin Books, 1969.

> One of the best of recent explorations of film aesthetics. In a clear and carefully organized discussion the authors touch on many important aesthetic questions.

Wolfenstein, Martha, and Leites, Nathan. Movies: A Psychological Study. Glencoe, Illinois: Free Press, 1950

> Although inconclusive, this extremely interesting study examines the relationship between the motion picture and its public. While more work remains to be done in this field, this provides an interesting and provocative starting point.

FILM PRODUCTION

Alton, John. Painting with Light. New York: The Macmillan Company, 1949.

> A highly interesting discussion of camera and lighting techniques from the studio point of view. Very well illustrated.

Baddeley, W. Hugh. The Technique of Documentary Film Production. New York: Hastings House, 1963

> Although purporting to deal with documentary film production, Baddeley's book serves as a complete introduction to all types of professional film production.

Carrick, Edward (pseudonym). Designing for Moving Pictures. London: Studio Publications, 1947.

> Unfortunately, few books are written which examine the problems of motion picture design. This one, while older, gives an excellent nontechnical account of the field.

Lawson, John H. Theory and Technique of Playwriting and Screenwriting. New York: G. P. Putnam's Sons, 1949.

> In earlier editions this work became a classic in the theatre field. Undoubtedly the most complete and meaningful examination of film writing.

Mascelli, Joseph V. The Five C's of Cinematography. Hollywood: Cine/Grafic Publications, 1966

> One of the most readable accounts of motion picture photographic techniques. Excellently illustrated with stills from many motion pictures.

Monier, Pierre. The Complete Technique of Making Films. New York: Ballantine Books, 1968.

> A widely read survey of motion picture production techniques. The completeness of the technical knowledge included makes this work of great value.

Nilsen, Vladimir. The Cinema as a Graphic Art. New York: Hill and Wang, 1959 (reprint).

> Despite the early date of its initial publication (1936), The Cinema as a Graphic Art remains one of the most stimulating discussions of the creative potentials of film production. Although limited in its range of examples, its examination of pictorial composition continues to be of immense value.

Reisz, Karel, and Millar, Gavin. The Technique of Film Editing. New York: Hastings House, 1967.

Although some of its examples are a bit obscure, no better examination of the problems and potentials of film editing exists. Provides a detailed examination of the editing of several film sequences.

Spottiswoode, Raymond. Film and Its Techniques. Berkeley: University of California Press, 1951.

Although somewhat outdated by post-1951 technology, Film and Its Techniques remains a complete and highly readable account of the film making process. It contains many excellent drawings and an extensive glossary of technical terms.

NATIONAL CINEMAS

Anderson, Joseph L., and Richie, Donald. The Japanese Film: Art and Industry. New York: Grove Press, 1959.

The oriental film has too often been virtually unknown in the West, despite the popularity of many recent Japanese motion pictures. This long and complex history of the art in Japan proved a revelation when it was published. A very complete and detailed study.

Hardy, Forsyth. Scandanavian Film. London: Falcon Press, 1952.

This account of the Scandanavian film is particularly valuable because American film historians have so often neglected to adequately examine the history of the Danish, Swedish, and Norwegian film. Although a brief account, it remains the standard introduction to Scandanavian motion pictures.

Kracauer, Siegfried. Caligari to Hitler: A Psychological History of the German Film. Princeton, New Jersey: Princeton University Press, 1966 (reprint).

The authoritative study of the early German film. This scholarly work, which ends in 1933, provides a very detailed examination of all important German films of the period.

Leyda, Jay. *Kino: A History of the Russian and Soviet Film.* New York: The Macmillan Company, 1960.

> The most widely read history of the Russian film. This study, which ends in 1947, provides many valuable insights into the problems of the early Russian film industry, in some cases actually observed by the author.

Low, Rachel. *The History of the British Film (1896-1906, 1906-1914, 1914-1918).* London: Allen and Unwin, 1948, 1949, 1950 (3 volumes).

> The first portion of what was to have been a complete examination of the history of the British film. Here the earliest and least known period of the British film is studied in detail.

Sadoul, Georges. *French Film.* London: Falcon Press, 1953.

> A brief but quite scholarly account of the French motion picture through World War II. An excellent introduction to this period of French film.

OTHER WORKS

Guback, Thomas H. *The International Film Industry: Western Europe and America Since 1945.* Bloomington, Indiana: Indiana University Press, 1969.

> Although information is available in trade journals, few books have attempted to examine the business and economic aspects of the film industry. This volume provides an immensely detailed, if somewhat dull examination of this aspect of film.

Huaco, George A. *The Sociology of Film Art.* New York: Basic Books, 1965.

> A standard work which has been examined with considerable interest. Unfortunately, it is limited in the film periods it discusses.

FILM RENTAL

It would be impossible to give an adequate description of the vast offerings of film rental agencies. These offerings are almost daily revised as new films are released for the rental market and as the contracts on older films expire.

From the standpoint of the scholar, American film rental agencies do offer many of the most significant Hollywood productions. The list of European films is more selective, but here again most films of interest are available. There are, however, many notable exceptions to the general availability of significant films: some films are withheld pending commercial reissues, others are involved in complex legal maneuvers, and still others are not offered because sufficient demand for them has not been demonstrated. The majority of all offerings are designed to appeal to a broad entertainment market, and thus new films are made available with amazing speed. Furthermore, the rapid growth of film courses in colleges and universities has increased the number of more significant films available for rental as well as the number of older films. It must be noted, however, that each year many older films which have not proved sufficiently popular are withdrawn.

Besides leading to the increased availability of films, the rapid growth of film courses has lead to a parallel rise in rental prices. Currently, feature length films rent from a low of about $25 to a high of about $350, depending upon the age and popularity of the film, with the majority renting for under $100. Some of the rental agencies listed below handle particular films on an exclusive basis, often demanding high prices. Most films, however, are available from a number of distributors, and thus one is able to shop competitively. Of value here is James Limbacher's <u>Feature Films on 8mm and 16mm: A Directory of Feature Films Available for Rental, Sale or Lease in the United States</u> (R. R. Bowker, 1971), although any printed volume is bound to become dated very quickly in a field which changes so rapidly. It is important to acquire regularly the catalogs of the agencies in order to keep abreast of current offerings and prices.

The list below includes distributors of short and experimental films as well as of feature length presentations. An * indicates a distributor of particularly valuable films.

FILM DISTRIBUTORS

Argosy Film Service
1939 Central Street
Evanston, Illinois 60201

Association-Sterling Films
600 Madison Avenue
New York, New York 10022

*Audio/Brandon Films, Inc.
    1619 North Cherokee
    Los Angeles, California 90028

    406 Clement Street
    San Francisco, California 94118

    512 Burlington Avenue
    La Grange, Illinois 60525

    34 MacQuesten Parkway S.
    Mount Vernon, New York 10550

    8615 Directors Row
    Dallas, Texas 75247

Canadian Film Makers Distribution Center
1 Charles Street E.
Toronto 5, Ontario, Canada

Canyon Cinema Cooperative
58 Verona Place
San Francisco, California 94107

Center Cinema Co-op
540 N. Lake Shore Drive
Chicago, Illinois 60611

Cine-Craft Company
709 S. W. Ankeny
Portland, Oregon 97205

Cine World
13 Arcadia Road
Old Greenwich, Connecticut   06870

Cinema Guild
10 Fiske Place
Mount Vernon, New York

Cinema 16
Grove Press Film Library
80 University Place
New York, New York   10003

*Columbia Cinematheque
711 Fifth Avenue
New York, New York   10022

*Contemporary Films, Inc.
       1211 Polk Street
       San Francisco, California   94109

       828 Custer Avenue
       Evanston, Illinois   60202

       267 W. 25th Street
       New York, New York   10001

Creative Film Society
14558 Valerio Street
Van Nuys, California

Embassy Pictures Corporation
1301 Avenue of the Americas
New York, New York   10019

EmGee Film Library
4931 Gloria Avenue
Encino, California   91316

Expanded Arts Center
GPO Box 1601
New York, New York   10001

Film Classic Exchange
1926 S. Vermont Avenue
Los Angeles, California   90007

Film Images
Radim Films, Inc.
    1034 Lake Street
    Oak Park, Illinois   60301

    17 W. 60th Street
    New York, New York   10023

Film Makers Cooperative
175 Lexington Avenue
New York, New York   10016

*Films Incorporated
    5625 Hollywood Boulevard
    Hollywood, California   90028

    3034 Canon Street
    San Diego, California   92106

    277 Pharr Road N. E.
    Atlanta, Georgia   30305

    4420 Oakton Street
    Skokie, Illinois   60076

    161 Massachusetts Avenue
    Boston, Massachusetts   02115

    35-01 Queens Boulevard
    Long Island City, New York   11101

    2129 N. E. Broadway
    Portland, Oregon   97232

    1414 Dragon Street
    Dallas, Texas   75207

    44 E. South Temple
    Salt Lake City, Utah   84110

Institutional Cinema Service
    1250 Ellis Street
    San Francisco, California   94109

    203 N. Wabash Avenue
    Chicago, Illinois   60601

    29 E. 10th Street
    New York, New York   10003

International Film Bureau
332 S. Michigan Avenue
Chicago, Illinois   60604

Ivy Film/16
120 E. 56th Street
New York, New York   10022

***Janus** Films
745 Fifth Avenue
New York, New York   10022

Joseph Burstyn, Inc.
200 W. 57th Street
New York, New York   10019

London Film Makers Cooperative
94 Charing Cross Road
London, W.C. 2, England

Mass Media Ministries
2116 N. Charles Street
Baltimore, Maryland   21218

Media International
107 N. Franklin Street
Madison, Wisconsin   53703

Mogull's
112 W. 48th Street
New York, New York   10019

*Museum of Modern Art
Department of Film
11 E. 53rd Street
New York, New York   10019

ROA Films
1696 N. Astor Street
Milwaukee, Wisconsin   53202

Rogosin Films
144 Bleecker Street
New York, New York   10012

Second City Center
1616 N. Wells Street
Chicago, Illinois   60614

Swank Motion Pictures
201 S. Jefferson
St. Louis, Missouri   63166

Trans-World Films, Inc.
332 S. Michigan Avenue
Chicago, Illinois   60604

Twyman Films, Inc.
329 Salem Avenue
Dayton, Ohio   45401

*United Artists 16
729 Seventh Avenue
New York, New York   10019

United World Films
542 S. Dearborn
Chicago, Illinois   60605

Universal Education and Visual Arts
221 Park Avenue S.
New York, New York   10003

Walt Disney Productions
800 Sonora Avenue
Glendale, California   91201

*Walter Reade 16
241 E. 34th Street
New York, New York 10016

*Warner Brothers 16
666 Fifth Avenue
New York, New York 10019

FILM PURCHASE

When a film must be examined for a prolonged period of time, rental often is not the most practical means of obtaining it for the researcher. Purchase of film copies then becomes highly attractive. Many of the great motion picture masterpieces of the silent era are now available, as well as some from the sound era. As the demand for scholarly access to films increases, we can hope that the scope of possible selections will also increase.

Films are available for purchase in 8mm and Super 8, as well as in 16mm. It is unfortunate that the list of available titles is shorter in 8mm and Super 8 than in 16mm, for 8mm and Super 8 are decidedly recommended. Eight millimeter film, while half the width of the more standard 16mm film, has only one-fourth the picture area. Thus a film acquired in an 8mm reduction print costs roughly only one-fourth as much as a 16mm print, with the result being that an entire feature length film may be acquired for thirty-five to fifty dollars. Eight millimeter and Super 8 films are very high quality today, and their optical characteristics improve each year. While 8mm film is not currently satisfactory for use in large auditoriums, it is certainly adequate for showing to smaller groups and for individual study. Improved projection equipment has virtually made 8mm projection indistinguishable from 16mm under normal conditions.

A list of recommended agencies and a highly selected list of films available for purchase appear below. Since some film titles are made available by collectors, the film list continually fluctuates. In cases in which sale rights have been withdrawn, sometimes a used copy will appear on the market. Prices will vary greatly depending upon market demand. Of some value to the potential film purchaser is Kalton C. Lahue's <u>Collecting Classic Films</u> (Hastings House, 1970): although oriented toward the private collector, it provides valuable information.

RECOMMENDED AGENCIES

Blackhawk Films
1235 W. Fifth Street
Davenport, Iowa   52808

Castle Films
221 Park Avenue S.
New York, New York   10003

Columbia Pictures
711 Fifth Avenue
New York, New York   10022

Edward Finney
1578 Queens Road
Hollywood, California   90069

Entertainment Film Company
850 Seventh Avenue
New York, New York   10019

Essex Film Club
263 Harrison Street
Nutley, New Jersey   07110

Film Classic Exchange
1926 S. Vermont Avenue
Los Angeles, California   90007

Griggs-Moviedrome
263 Harrison Street
Nutley, New Jersey   07110

I. K. Meginnis
Box 5803
Washington, D. C.   20014

Movie Classics of the Silver
  Screen
P. O. Box 1463
Philadelphia, Pennsylvania
  19105

Nick Fiorentino
60-B Newark Way
Maplewood, New Jersey   07040

Sears Roebuck Company
All cities

Willoughby/Peerless Film
  Library
115 W. 31st Street
New York, New York   10001

SELECTED LIST OF FILMS AVAILABLE FOR PURCHASE

The Birth of a Nation

The Black Pirate

Blood and Sand

Broken Blossoms

The Cabinet of Dr. Caligari

The Circus

City Lights

Don Juan

Foolish Wives

The General

The Gold Rush

The Golem

The Good Earth

Great Expectations

The Great Train Robbery

Hamlet

The Hunchback of Notre Dame

The Informer

Judith of Bethulia

The Kid

King Kong

The Last Laugh

The Lost World

M

Manhandled

Metropolis

Modern Times

The Music Box

Nanook of the North

Never Give a Sucker an Even Break

Nosferatu

Open City

Orphans of the Storm

The Passion of Joan of Arc

Phantom of the Opera

Potemkin

The Road to Yesterday

Salome

Son of the Sheik

The Story of Gosta Berling

Sunrise

Tarzan of the Apes

Ten Days that Shook the World

Thief of Baghdad

Tillie's Punctured Romance

Tol'able David

The Tramp

A Trip to the Moon

Triumph of the Will

Tumbleweeds

Two Tars

Variety

The Virgin Spring

Way Down East

When Worlds Collide

FILM PERIODICALS

The following periodicals might prove useful to researchers.

A B C Film Review
Cinemas and Leisure Ltd.
30-31 Golden Square
London W. 1, England

A V Communication Review
Association for Educational Communications and Technology
1201 16th Street N. W.
Washington, D. C.   20036

Action
Directors Guild of America
7950 Sunset Boulevard
Hollywood, California   90046

American Cinematographer
American Society of Cinematographers Agency, Inc.
1782 North Orange Drive
Los Angeles, California   90028

Audience
Wilson Associates
866 Carroll Street
Brooklyn, New York   11215

Audiovisual Instruction
National Education Association
1201 16th Street N. W.
Washington, D. C.   20036

Audio-Visual Marketing News
General Publishing
7061 Hayvenhurst Avenue
Van Nuys, California   91406

Bianco e Nero
Edizioni di Bianco e Nero
Via Tuscolana 1524
Rome, Italy

Bild und Ton
VEB Fotokinoverlag Leipzig
Karl-Heine-Str. 16
Leipzig, East Germany

Box Office
Associated Publications
825 Van Brunt Boulevard
Kansas City, Missouri   64124

British Kinematography, Sound and Television
British Kinematograph Sound and Television Society
110-112 Victoria House
Vernon Place
London, W. C. 1, England

Bulgarian Films
State Film Distribution
135 Rakovsky Str.
Sofia, Bulgaria

Business Screen
Harcourt, Brace, Jovanovich
402 West Liberty Drive
Wheaton, Illinois   60187

Cahiers du Cinema
8 rue Marbeuf
Paris (8e), France

Canadian Film Digest
Film Publications of Canada Ltd.
175 Bloor Street E.
Toronto 5, Ontario, Canada

Canyon Cinemanews
Industrial Center Building, Room 220
Sausalito, California 94965

Catholic Film Newsletter
National Catholic Office for Motion Pictures
405 Lexington Avenue, Suite 4200
New York, New York 10017

Cine al Dia
Sociedad Civil Cine al Dia
Apartado 50 446, Sabana Grande
Caracas, Venezuela

Cine Camera
Federation of Canadian Amateur Cinematographers
Box 273, Youville Station
Montreal 351, P.q., Canada

Cine Cubano
1155 Calle 23, Vedado
Havana, Cuba

Cine World
Box 86
Toronto 9, Canada

Cineaste
144 Bleecker Street
New York, New York 10012

Cineforum
Federazione Italiana Cineforum
Casella Postale 414
Venice, Italy

Cinema
9667 Wilshire Boulevard
Beverly Hills, California   90212

Cinema Canada
Canadian Society of Cinematographers
2533 Gerrald Street E.
Scarborough, Ontario, Canada

Cinema Journal
Society for Cinema Studies
21 Maple Avenue
Bridgewater, Massachusetts   02324

Cinema Pratique
Editions Technique Europeennes
45 rue St. Roch
Paris (1er), France

Cinema Societa
Via Monte Cervialto 102
Rome, Italy

Cinematografia Ita
Via Baiamonti 10
Rome, Italy

Cinestudio
Hermosilla 20
Madrid 1, Spain

Classic Film Collector
734 Philadelphia Street
Indiana, Pennsylvania   15701

Communications Arts International
Leeward Publications
Box 2801
Washington, D. C.   20013

Continental Film Review
Eurap Publishing Company Ltd.
71 Oldhill Street
London N. 16, England

Critic
Film Critics' Guild
9 Compayne Gardens
London N. W. 6, England

Czechoslovak Film
Vaclavske nam. 28
Prague 1, Czechoslovakia

Daily Variety
6404 Sunset Boulevard
Hollywood, California 90028

Educational Screen and Audio Visual Guide
Trade Periodicals, Inc.
434 S. Wabash
Chicago, Illinois 60605

Fantasy Film Review
10 Dartmouth Avenue
Oldfield Park, Bath BA 2 IAT
Somerset, England

Fernseh und Filmtechnikum
Kommanditgesellschaft Verlag Horst
Axtmann GmbH, Wilhelmstr. 42
Wiesbaden, West Germany

Film
Kirke og Film
Ellevadsvej 4
Charl., Denmark

Film
British Federation of Film Societies
81 Dean Street
London W. 1, England

Film
Wydawnictwa Artystyczne Filmowe
Pulawska 61
Warsaw, Poland

Film
3001 Velber
Hannover, West Germany

Film and Television Daily
Wid's Films and Film Folk, Inc.
1600 Broadway
New York, New York 10019

Film and Television Technician
Association of Cinematograph, Television and Allied Technicians
2 Soho Square
London W. 1, England

Film Bulletin
Wax Publications, Inc.
1239 Vine Street
Philadelphia, Pennsylvania 19107

Film Comment
100 Walnut Place
Brookline, Massachusetts 02146

Film Culture
Box 1499, G. P. O.
New York, New York 10001

Film Fan Monthly
77 Grayson Place
Teaneck, New Jersey 07666

Film Francais--Cinematographie Francaise
28 rue Bayard
Paris (8e), France

Film Heritage
University of Dayton
Box 652
Dayton, Ohio 45409

Film Index
10-2e Mosman Street
Mosman Bay, Australia

Film Information
Broadcasting and Film Commission
National Council of Churches
Box 500, Manhattanville Station
New York, New York   10027

Film Italiano
Unitalia Film
Via Veneto 108
Rome, Italy

Film Library Quarterly
Film Library Information Council
17 W. 60th Street
New York, New York   10023

Film Making Magazine
Haymarket Publishing Ltd.
Winsley Street
London W. 1, England

Film News
250 W. 57th Street
New York, New York   10019

Film Quarterly
University of California Press
Berkeley, California   94720

Film Roumain/Romanian Film
Romania Film
25, Julius Fucik Street
Bucharest, Romania

Film Society Review
American Federation of Film Societies
144 Bleecker Street
New York, New York   10012

Film User
Current Affairs Ltd.
Box 109
Croydon, Surrey CR9 2QH, England

Film Weekly
Derwent Enterprises Pty. Ltd.
340 Pitt Street
Sydney 2000, Australia

Film World
Film World International Publications Private Ltd.
A-15, anand Nagar, Juhu Tara Road
Bombay 54, India

Filmcritica
Via Carlo Fea 6
Rome, Italy

Filme Cultura
Instituto Nacional do Cinma
Rua 20 de Abril, 28
2 Andar, Sala 201, Centro
Rio de Janeiro, Brazil

Filmfacts
American Film Institute
Box 213, Village Station
New York, New York   10014

Filmkultura
Magyar Filmtudomanyi Intezet
Nepstadion ut 97
Budapest 14, Hungary

Filmlist
Education Film Library Association
17 W. 60th Street
New York, New York   10023

Filmmakers' Newsletter
Box 46
New York, New York   10012

Films and Filming
Hansom Books
Artillery Mansions
75 Victoria Street
London S. W. 1, England

Films in Review
National Board of Review of Motion Pictures, Inc.
210 E. 68th Street
New York, New York   10021

Filmtheater-Praxis
Kommanditgesellschaft Verlag Horst Axtmann GmbH und Co.
Wilhelmstr. 42
Wiesbaden, West Germany

Focus on Film
Tantivy Press
108 New Bond Street
London W. 1, England

Foto-Kino Revija
Technicka Knjiga
7 Jula Br. 26
Belgrade, Yugoslavia

Hollywood Screen Parade
Actual Publishing Company
95 Madison Avenue
New York, New York   10016

Hungarofilm Bulletin
Hungarofilm
V. Bathory u. lo.
Budapest, Hungary

Independent Film Journal
165 W. 46th Street
New York, New York   10036

Indian Movie News
Chinese Pictorial Review Ltd.
112-120 Robinson Road
Singapore

International Motion Picture Exhibitor
Shain Enterprises, Inc.
1600 Broadway
New York, New York   10019

Interview
33 Union Square W.
New York, New York   10003

Iskusstvo Kino
Soyuz Rabotnikov Kinematografii SSSR
ul. Usiyevicha 9
Moscow A-319, USSR

Italian Production
Unitalia Film
Via Veneto 108
Rome, Italy

Kine Weekly
Specialist and Professional Press Ltd.
161-166 Fleet Street
London EC4P 4AA, England

Kino
Wydawnictwa Artystyczne i Filmowe
ul. Pulawska 61
Warsaw, Poland

Kinotechnik
Wydawnictwa Artystyezne i Filmowe
ul. Pulawska 61
Warsaw, Poland

Media and Methods
134 N. 13th Street
Philadelphia, Pennsylvania   19107

Medium
Filmage, Inc.
18 Centre Street
New York, New York   10013

Motion Picture Daily
Quigley Publishing Company
1270 Sixth Avenue
New York, New York   10020

Motion Picture Herald
Quigley Publishing Co.
1270 Sixth Avenue
New York, New York 10020

Motion Picture Magazine
Macfadden-Bartell Corporation
205 E. 42nd Street
New York, New York 10017

Movie
Movie Magazine Ltd.
3 Cork Street
London W. 1, England

Movie Life
Ideal Publishing Corporation
295 Madison Avenue
New York, New York 10017

Movie Maker
Fountain Press Ltd.
46-47 Chancery Lane
London W.C. 2, England

Movie Mirror
Sterling Group, Inc.
315 Park Avenue S.
New York, New York 10010

Movie News
600 George Street
Sydney, N. S. W. 2000, Australia

Movie Stars
Ideal Publishing Corporation
295 Madison Avenue
New York, New York 10017

Movie World
Magazine Management Company
625 Madison Avenue
New York, New York 10022

Movies
Vanity Fair
5512 Wayne Avenue
Philadelphia, Pennsylvania   19144

New Cinema Review
Box 34
New York, New York   10012

Nouveau Cinema Canadien/New Canadian Film
Cinematheque Canadienne
3834 ru Staint Denis
Montreal 131, Quebec, Canada

Nouveau Cinemonde
Societe Francaise d'Editions et de Publications Illustrees
2a 12 rue de Bellevue
Paris (19e), France

Nuestro Cine
Santiago de la Heras, Macarena
Madrid 16, Spain

Photoplay
Macfadden-Bartell Corporation
205 E. 42nd Street
New York, New York   10017

Picturegoer
Picturegoer Publications
92 Daryaganj
Delhi, India

Polish Film/Film Polonais
Film Polski-Export and Import of Films
ul., Mazowiecka 6/8
Warsaw, Poland

Presence du Cinema
25 Passage des Princes
Paris (2e), France

Revue du Cinema/Image et Son
Lique Francaise de l'Enseignement
3 rue Recamier
Paris (E), France

Screen
Society for Education in Film and Television
81 Dean Street
London W. 1, England

Screen Facts
123-40 83rd Avenue
Kew Gardens, New York   11415

Screenland
Macfadden-Bartell Corporation
205 E. 42nd Street
New York, New York   10017

See
George A. Pflaum
38 W. Fifth Street
Dayton, Ohio   45402

Segnalazioni Cinematografiche
Via della Conciliazione, 2-C
Rome 00193, Italy

Show
Show Publications, Inc.
866 United Nations Plaza
New York, New York   10017

Sight and Sound
British Film Institute
81 Dean Street
London WIV AA, England

Sightlines
Educational Film Library Association
17 W. 60th Street
New York, New York   10023

Silent Picture
613 Harrow Road
London W. 10, England

Silver Screen
Macfadden-Bartell Corporation
205 E. 42nd Street
New York, New York   10017

SMPTE Journal
Society of Motion Picture and Television Engineers
9 E. 41st Street
New York, New York   10017

Society of Film and Television Arts Journal
80 Great Portland Street
London W1N 6JJ, England

Sovetskoye Kino
Mezhdunarodnaya Kniga
Smolenskaya Sennaya 32 34
Moscow G-200, USSR

Soviet Film/Sovetski Film
Mezhdunarodnaya Kniga
Smolenskaya Sennaya 32 34
Moscow G-200, USSR

Take One
Box 1778, Station B
Montreal 110, Quebec, Canada

Tiempo de Cine
Cineclub Nucleo & Lavalle 2016
80 piso of 17
Buenos Aires, Argentina

Unijapan Film Quarterly
Association for the Diffusion of Japanese Films Abroad
Nakamura Building
9-13 Ginza 5-chome, Chuo-ku
Tokyo 104, Japan

University Film Association Journal
Department of Photography and Cinema
The Ohio State University
156 W. 19th Avenue
Columbus, Ohio   43210

Variety
154 W. 46th Street
New York, New York   10036

USING THE BIBLIOGRAPHY

The major bibliography has been divided into sections to facilitate its use. It is important to understand the composition of the various categories in order to locate the desired material as quickly as possible.

Category 1: Film History, Theory, Criticism and Introductory Works. This is one of the two largest categories in the bibliography. It is frequently difficult to separate film history and film theory since many volumes attempt to discuss both. Moreover, some critical works are also partially historical or theoretical. And introductory works frequently touch on all areas of film. For these reasons all of these works have been grouped together. The section contains film production books written from an analytical or spectator's point of view. A few volumes about film direction are included too, since they can serve as introductory works. And a few biographies are included because of the historical and critical insights they offer.

Categories 2 and 3: Film Production and Technology--I and II. Volumes concerned with film production from a practitioner's viewpoint are contained in these two categories. Their subject area consists of works on film writing, acting, photography, editing, sound, and other production aspects of the motion picture. Also included are works which examine technological areas and works which deal with architecture for the motion picture theatre. Category 2 contains recent works and older works whose content is still accurate, while Category 3 contains older works which no longer accurately describe film production methods but which are, nonetheless, of historical interest.

Category 4: Film Genre consists of all works about special types of film, from the animation to the western.

Category 5: Sociology and Economics of Film. This section of the bibliography examines the social and economic aspects of the motion picture. Included here are works concerned with the effect of the motion picture on society, volumes on censorship, examinations of many business and economic aspects of the film industry, psychological studies of the motion picture, and works concerned with political and legal aspects of film.

Category 6: National Cinemas includes volumes devoted to a study of the films and film industries of various countries, excluding the United States.

Category 7: <u>Film Scripts</u> lists both individual volumes and anthologies of film scripts.

Category 8: <u>Particular Films</u> consists of volumes which are devoted to the study of specific motion pictures. These books are of various types. Many are production logs of motion pictures, others give background information, some are summaries of research conducted, and some deal with one special aspect of a film. When the identity of the film under discussion is not clear from the title of the book, it is indicated in parentheses following the publication data.

Category 9: <u>Personalities, Biographies, and Filmographies.</u> This portion of the bibliography lists a wide variety of works. It includes biographies and autobiographies, studies of individual filmmakers, pictorial histories of the careers of various individuals, and scholarly studies of film personalities, as well as books about various curious aspects of motion pictures. This lengthy section contains, in short, any work dealing with the films and/or career of one individual or group.

Category 10: <u>Film Education</u> includes textbooks suitable for use in elementary and secondary schools, works about the teaching of film, volumes concerned with the use of film in education, and discussions of film applications in business and industrial settings. When a work is intended for use with a particular nonadult age group, the level of that group is indicated in parentheses following the publication data.

Category 11: Film-Related Works consists of volumes which, while not specifically about film, contain some film material or include discussions of interest to film researchers.

Category 12: Careers in Film includes works which examine film as a career field.

Category 13: Bibliographies, Guides, and Indexes. Listed in this section are all types of film reference books.

Category 14: Selected Works in Foreign Languages. This category includes many volumes available only in foreign languages. There is a great deal of very significant cinema literature which is not available in English. Of this mass of literature, a selection has been made for inclusion here. Special emphasis has been placed on the most valuable works available in major European languages. While most of these works are in French or Italian, a considerable amount of untranslated cinema literature is available in virtually every language.

Many of the broad works in the bibliography have been listed in several appropriate categories.

In the material which follows all data have been indicated in a somewhat abridged form to facilitate rapid use of the bibliography. The symbol (rp.) indicates reprinted material.

THE MAJOR BIBLIOGRAPHY

CATEGORY 1: FILM HISTORY, THEORY, CRITICISM AND INTRODUCTORY WORKS

Ackland, Rodney and Elspeth Grant
The Celluloid Mistress, or the Custard Pie of Dr. Caligari
London: Allen Wingate, 1954

Acting for Film
See Category 2: Film Production and Technology I--Contemporary

Adler, Mortimer J.
Art and Prudence: A Study in Practical Philosophy
N.Y.: Columbia Teachers College Press, 1965

Adler, Renata
A Year in the Dark
N.Y.: Random House, 1969

Agate, James
Around Cinemas
London: Home & Von Thal, 1946

Agate, James
Around Cinemas--Second Series
London: Home & Von Thal, 1948

Agate, James
On an English Screen
N.Y.: Benjamin Blom, (rp.)

Agee, James
Agee on Film
Vol. 1: Reviews and Comments
Boston: Beacon, 1964

Allen, Kenneth S.
The Silver Screen
London: J. Gifford, 1948

Alloway, Lawrence
Violent America: The Movies 1946-1964
N.Y.: Museum of Modern Art, 1971

Alpert, Hollis
The Dreams and the Dreamers
N.Y.: Macmillan, 1962

Altshuler, Thelma and Richard P. Janaro
Responses to Drama: An Introduction to Plays and Movies
Boston: Houghton Mifflin, 1967

Anderson, John and Rene Fulop-Miller
American Theater and The Motion Picture in America
N.Y.: Johnson Reprint Corp., 1970 (rp.)

Anderson, Milton (pseud.)
The Modern Goliath
L.A.: David Press, 1935

Andrews, Cyril B.
The Theatre, the Cinema, and
  Ourselves
London: Clarence House Press,
  1947

Animated Films
  See Category 4: Film Genre

Anstey, Edgar, Roger Manvell,
  Ernest Lindgren and Paul
  Rotha
Shots in the Dark
London: Blumenthal, Gitta Allan
  Wingate, 1951

Arnheim, Rudolph
Art and Visual Perception: A
  Psychology of the Creative Eye
Berkeley: U. of Cal. Press, 1954

Arnheim, Rudolph
Film
London: Faber, 1933

Arnheim, Rudolph
Film as Art
Berkeley: U. of Cal. Press, 1957

Art of Cinema
N.Y.: Kraus Reprint Co.,
  (rp.)

The Art of Cinema: Selected
  Essays
N.Y.: Arno, 1971

Austin, John
Hollywood's Unsolved Mysteries
N.Y.: Ace, 1970

Balázs, Béla
Theory of the Film
N.Y.: Roy Pubs., 1953

Bardèche, Maurice and Robert
  Brasillach
The History of Motion Pictures
N.Y.: Arno, 1970 (rp.)

Bare, Richard L.
The Film Director
N.Y.: Macmillan, 1971

Barry, Iris
Let's Go to the Movies
London: Chatto & Windus, 1926

Battcock, Gregory (ed.)
The New American Cinema: A
  Critical Anthology
N.Y.: Dutton, 1967

Baxter, John
Hollywood in the Thirties
N.Y.: Barnes, 1968

Bazin, André
What Is Cinema?
Berkeley: U. of Cal. Press, 1967

Bazin, André
What Is Cinema? (Vol. 2)
Berkeley: U. of Cal. Press, 1971

Beaton, Welford
Know Your Movies
L.A.: Howard Hill, 1932

Beckoff, Samuel
Motion Pictures
N.Y.: Oxford Bk. Co., 1953

Bellone, Julius (ed.)
The Renaissance of the Film
N.Y.: Macmillan, 1970

Bendick, Jeanne and Robert Bendick
Filming Works Like This
N.Y.: McGraw-Hill, 1970

Bennett, Alfred G.
Cinemania: Aspects of Filmic Creation
London: Garrolds, 1937

Benoit-Lévy, Jean
The Art of the Motion Picture
N.Y.: Arno, 1970 (rp.)

Betts, Ernest
Heraclitus or The Future of Films
N.Y.: Dutton, 1928

Betts, Ernest
Inside Pictures: With Some Reflections from the Outside
London: Cresset Press, 1960

Bird, John H.
Cinema Parade: Fifty Years of Film Shows
Birmingham, England: Cornish Bros., 1947

Blakeston, Oswell
Working for the Films
London: Focal Press, 1947

Bluestone, George
Novels into Film
Berkeley: U. of Cal. Press, 1966

Blum, Daniel C.
A New Pictorial History of the Talkies
N.Y.: G. P. Putnam's Sons, 1968

Blum, Daniel C.
A Pictorial History of the Silent Screen
N.Y.: G. P. Putnam's Sons, 1953

Blum, Daniel C.
A Pictorial History of the Talkies
N.Y.: Grosset & Dunlap, 1958

Bobker, Lee R.
Elements of Film
N.Y.: Harcourt, Brace & World, 1969

Bowser, Eileen
Film Notes, Part I
N.Y.: Museum of Modern Art, 1969

Boyd, Malcolm
Christ and Celebrity Gods: The Church in Mass Culture
Greenwich, Conn.: Seabury Press, 1958

Boyum, Joy G. and Adrienne Scott
Film a Film: Critical Responses to Film Art
Boston: Allyn & Bacon, 1971

British Film Institute: National Film Theatre
Fifty Famous Films 1915-1945
London: British Film Inst., 1960

British Film Institute
The First Twenty-five Years
London: British Film Inst., 1958

Brownlow, Kevin
The Parade's Gone by
N.Y.: Alfred A. Knopf, 1968

Bryne-Daniel, Jack
Grafilm: An Approach to a New
  Medium
N.Y.: Van Nostrand Reinhold,
  1970

Buchanan, Andrew
Film and the Future
London: George Allen & Unwin,
  1945

Buchanan, Andrew
Films: The Way of the Cinema
London: I. Pitman & Sons, 1932

Buckle, Fort G.
The Mind and the Film
N.Y.: Arno, 1970 (rp.)

Butler, Ivan
The Making of Feature Films--A
  Guide
Baltimore: Penguin, 1971

Cairn, James
The Heart of Hollywood
London: D.S. Smith, 1945

Callenbach, Ernest
Our Modern Art, the Movies
Chicago: Center for Study of
  Liberal Education for Adults,
  1955

Cameron, Ian
Movie Reader
N.Y.: Praeger, 1971

Carey, Gary
Lost Films
N.Y.: Museum of Modern Art,
  1970

Carter, Huntly
The New Spirit in the Cinema
N.Y.: Arno, 1970 (rp.)

Casty, Alan
The Dramatic Art of the Film
N.Y.: Harper & Row, 1971

Ceram, C.W. (pseud.)
Archaeology of Cinema
N.Y.: Harcourt, Brace & World,
  1965

Charlot, Jean
Art from the Mayans to Disney
N.Y.: Sheed & Ward, 1939

Chesmore, Stuart
Behind the Cinema Screen
London: T. Nelson & Sons, 1935

Cinema Commission of Inquiry
The Cinema: Its Present Position
  and Future Possibilities
N.Y.: Arno, 1970 (rp.)

Cinematography
   See Category 2: Film Produc-
      tion and Technology I--Con-
      temporary

Cinema verité
   See Category 4: Film Genre

Clair, René
Reflections on the Cinema
London: W. Kimber, 1953

Clark, Henry
Academy Award Diary, 1928-
  1955: A Motion Picture History
N.Y.: Pageant Press, 1959

Cocteau, Jean
Cocteau on the Film, a Conversation Recorded by André Fraigneau
N.Y.: Roy Pubs., 1954

Cocteau, Jean
Screenplays and Other Writings on the Cinema
N.Y.: Orion, 1968

Comedy Films
See Category 4: Film Genre

Contemporary Film
N.Y.: Assn. Press, 1970

Cooke, David C.
Behind the Scenes in Motion Pictures
N.Y.: Dodd, Mead, 1960

Cooper, John C. and Carl Skrade (eds.)
Celluloid and Symbols
Philadelphia: Fortress Press, 1970

Cowie, Peter (ed.)
A Concise History of the Cinema (2 vols.)
N.Y.: Barnes, 1970

Cowie, Peter
Seventy Years of Cinema
N.Y.: Barnes, 1969

Crist, Judith
The Private Eye, the Cowboy and the Very Naked Girl
N.Y.: Paperback Lib., 1967

Crowther, Bosley
The Great Films: Fifty Golden Years of Motion Pictures
N.Y.: G. P. Putnam's Sons, 1967

Crowther, Bosley
Hollywood Rajah: The Life and Times of Louis B. Mayer
N.Y.: Holt, Rinehart & Winston, 1960

Crowther, Bosley
The Lion's Share
N.Y.: Dutton, 1957

Croy, Homer
How Motion Pictures Are Made
N.Y.: Harper & Bros., 1918

Crump, Irving
Our Movie Makers
N.Y.: Dodd, Mead, 1940

Curti, Carlo
Skouras: King of Fox Studios
L.A.: Holloway House, 1967

Dadoul, Georges
British Creators of Film Technique: British Scenario Writers, the Creators of the Language of D. W. Griffith, G. A. Smith, Alfred Collins, and Some Others
London: British Film Inst., 1948

Dale, Edgar
The Content of Motion Pictures
N.Y.: Arno, 1970 (rp.)

Dale, Edgar
How to Appreciate Motion Pictures
N.Y.: Arno, 1970 (rp.)

Davy, Charles (ed.)
Footnotes to the Film
N.Y.: Arno, 1970 (rp.)

Day, Beth
This Was Hollywood: An Affectionate History of Filmland's Golden Years
Garden City, N.Y.: Doubleday, 1960

De Bartolo, Dick, et al
A Mad Look at Old Movies
N.Y.: New American Lib., 1966

De Bartolo, Dick, et al
Return of Mad Look at Old Movies
N.Y.: New American Lib.,

Deming, Barbara
Running Away from Myself: A Dream Portrait of America Drawn from the Films of the Forties
N.Y.: Grossman, 1969

Dench, Ernest A.
Making the Movies
N.Y.: Macmillan, 1915

Design for Film
See Category 2: Film Production and Technology I--Contemporary

Dickinson, Thorold
Discovery of Cinema
Fair Lawn, N.J.: Oxford U. Press, 1971

Dickson, W.K.L. and Antonia Dickson
History of the Kinetograph, Kinetoscope and Kinetophonograph
N.Y.: Arno, 1970 (rp.)

Direction in Film
Also see Category 2: Film Production and Technology I--Contemporary

Documentary Film
See Category 4: Film Genre

Douglas, Kenneth (ed.)
Yale French Studies: Art of the Cinema
New Haven, Conn.: Yale U. Press, 1956

Dunne, John G.
The Studio
N.Y.: Farrar, Straus & Giroux, 1969

Durgnat, Raymond
Film and Feelings
Cambridge, Mass.: MIT Press, 1967

Eisenstein, Sergei
Film Essays
London: Dennis Dobson, 1968

Eisenstein, Sergei
Film Essays with a Lecture
N.Y.: Praeger, 1970

Eisenstein, Sergei
Film Form and Film Sense
Cleveland: World Pub. Co., 1957

Experimental Films
See Category 4: Film Genre

Eyles, Allen and Pat Billings
Hollywood Today
Cranbury, N.J.: Barnes, 1971

Farber, Manny
Negative Space: Twenty-Five Years at the Movies
N.Y.: Praeger, 1971

Faure, Elie
The Art of Cineplastics
Boston: Four Seas, 1923

Faure, Elie
The Art of Cineplastics
Reissued in Screen Monographs I. N.Y.: Arno, 1970

Fawcett, L'Estrange
Films: Facts and Forecasts
Boston: G. Bles, 1927

Fay, Arthur
Bioscope Shows and Their Engines
Lingfield, Sy., England: Oakwood Press, 1966

Feldman, Joseph and Harry Feldman
Dynamics of the Film
N.Y.: Heritage House, 1952

Fenderson, Julia K.
Let's Visit a Movie Lot
Culver City, Cal.: Board of Education, 1956

Fensch, Thomas
Films on the Campus
N.Y.: Barnes, 1970

Field, Alice E.
Hollywood, U.S.A., from Script to Screen
N.Y.: Vantage Press, 1952

Field, Robert D.
The Art of Walt Disney
N.Y.: Macmillan, 1942

Fielding, Raymond
A Technological History of Motion Pictures and Television
Berkeley: U. of Cal. Press, 1967

Film Council of America
Sixty Years of 16mm Film, 1923-1983
Evanston, Ill.: Film Council of America, 1954

Fischer, Edward
The Screen Arts: A Guide to Film and Television Appreciation
N.Y.: Sheed & Ward, 1960

Fletcher, John G.
The Crisis of the Film
Reissued in Screen Monographs II. N.Y.: Arno, 1970

Floherty, John J.
Moviemakers
N.Y.: Doubleday, Doran, 1935

Franklin, Joe
Classics of the Silent Screen
N.Y.: Citadel, 1959

Frederik, Nathalie
Hollywood and the Academy Awards
N.Y.: Ace, 1970

Freeburg, Victor O.
The Art of Photoplay Making
N.Y.: Arno, 1970 (rp.)

Freeburg, Victor O.
Pictorial Beauty on the Screen
N.Y.: Arno Press, 1970 (rp.)

French, Philip
The Movie Moguls: An Informal History of the Hollywood Tycoons
London: Weidenfeld & Nicolson, 1969

Freulich, R. and J. Abramson
Forty Years in Hollywood: Portraits of a Golden Age
Cranbury, N.J.: Barnes, 1971

Fulton, Albert R.
Motion Pictures: The Development of an Art from the Silent Films to the Age of Television
Norman, Okla.: U. of Okla. Press, 1960

Furhammar, L. and F. Isaksson
Politics and Film
N.Y.: Praeger, 1971

Gangster Films
    See Category 4: Film Genre

Gardiner, Harold C. and Moira Walsh
Tenets for Movie Viewers
N.Y.: America Press, 1962

Geduld, Harry M. (ed.)
Film Makers on Film Making
Bloomington, Ind.: Ind. U. Press, 1968

Gelmis, Joseph
The Film Director as Superstar
Garden City, N.Y.: Doubleday, 1970

Gessner, Robert
The Moving Image: A Guide to Cinematic Literacy
N.Y.: Dutton, 1968

Giannetti, Louis D.
Understanding Movies
Englewood Cliffs, N.J.: Prentice-Hall, 1972

Gilbert, Dan
What Is Happening in Hollywood
L.A.: Jewish Hope Pub. House, 194?

Goldwyn, Samuel
Behind the Screen
N.Y.: George H. Doran, 1923

Goodman, Ezra
The Fifty Year Decline and Fall of Hollywood
N.Y.: Simon & Schuster, 1961

Gordon, Bernard and Julian Zimet
The Technique of Film
Reissued in Screen Monographs I. N.Y.: Arno, 1970

Gordon, Jan & Cora Gordon
Star-Dust in Hollywood
London: G. G. Harrap & Co., 1931

Gow, Gordon
Hollywood in the Fifties
Cranbury, N.J.: Barnes, 1971

Graham, Peter
A Dictionary of the Cinema
N.Y.: Barnes, 1964

Grau, Robert
The Theatre of Science
N.Y.: Benjamin Blom, (rp.)

Green, Abel and Joe Laurie, Jr.
Show Biz
N.Y.: Holt, Rinehart & Winston, 1951

Green, Fitzhugh
The Film Finds Its Tongue
N.Y.: G.P. Putnam's Sons, 1929

Gregg, Eugene S.
Shadow of Sound
N.Y.: Vantage Press, 1968

Grey, Elizabeth B.
Behind the Scenes in a Film Studio
N.Y.: Roy Pubs., 1968

Griffith, Mrs. D.W. (Linda Arvidson)
When the Movies Were Young
N.Y.: Benjamin Blom, 1968 (rp.)

Griffith, Richard
Samuel Goldwyn: The Producer and His Films
N.Y.: Simon & Schuster, 1956

Griffith, Richard and Arthur Mayer
The Movies: The Sixty Year Story of the World of Hollywood and Its Effect on America
N.Y.: Simon & Schuster, 1957

Guback, Thomas H.
The International Film Industry: Western Europe and America Since 1945
Bloomington, Ind.: Ind. U. Press, 1969

Halliwell, Leslie
The Filmgoer's Companion: From Nickelodeon to the New Wave
N.Y.: Hill & Wang, 1967

Hampton, Benjamin B.
History of the American Film Industry from the Beginnings to 1931
N.Y.: Dover Pubs., 1970

Hampton, Benjamin B.
A History of the Movies
N.Y.: Arno, 1970 (rp.)

Handel, Leo A.
Hollywood Looks at Its Audience
Urbana, Ill.: U. of Ill., 1950

Hannon, William M.
The Photodrama
Reissued in Screen Monographs II. N.Y.: Arno, 1970

Harcourt, Peter and Peter Theobald (eds.)
Film Making in Schools and Colleges
London: British Film Inst., 1966

Harmon, Francis S.
The Command Is Forward: Selections from Addresses on the Motion Picture Industry in War and Peace
N.Y.: R.R. Smith, 1944

Haskin, Dorothy
Behind the Scenes in Hollywood
Grand Rapids, Mich.: Zondervan, 1951

Hauser, Arnold
The Social History of Art: Volume 4
N.Y.: Vintage Bks., 1951

Hays, Will H.
Motion Pictures: An Outline of the History and Achievements of the Screen from Its Earliest Beginnings to the Present Day
N.Y.: Doubleday, Doran, 1929

Hays, Will H.
See and Hear
Reissued in Screen Monographs II. N.Y.: Arno, 1970

Henderson, Robert
D. W. Griffith: The Years at Biograph
N.Y.: Farrar, Straus & Giroux, 1970

Henderson, Ron (ed.)
Image Maker
Richmond, Va.: John Knox Press, 1971

Hendricks, Gordon
Beginnings of the Biograph
N.Y.: Beginnings of the American Film, 1964

Hendricks, Gordon
The Edison Motion Picture Myth
Berkeley: U. of Cal. Press, 1961

Hendricks, Gordon
The Kinetoscope: America's First Commercially Successful Motion Picture Exhibitor
N.Y.: Beginnings of the American Film, 1966

Herring, Robert, Bryher (pseud.), and Dallas Bower
Cinema Survey
London: Brendin Pub. Co., 1937

Higham, Charles and Joel Greenberg
Hollywood in the Forties
N.Y.: Barnes, 1968

Hill, Laurance L. and Silas E. Snyder
Can Anything Good Come out of Hollywood?
L.A.: Times-Mirror Press, 1923

Hogben, Lancelot
From Cave Painting to Comic Strip: A Kaleidoscope of Human Communication
N.Y.: Chanticleer Press, 1949

Holaday, Perry W. and George D. Stoddard
Getting Ideas from the Movies
N.Y.: Arno, 1970 (rp.)

Hollander, John
Movie-Going
N.Y.: Atheneum Pubs., 1962

Hopwood, Henry V.
Living Pictures: Their History, Photo-Production and Practical Working
N.Y.: Arno, 1970 (rp.)

Horror Films
See Category 4: Film Genre

Hound and Horn: Essays on Cinema
N.Y.: Arno, 1971

Houston, Penelope
The Contemporary Cinema
Baltimore: Penguin, 1963

Huaco, George A.
The Sociology of Film Art
N.Y.: Basic Bks., 1965

Hughes, Langston and Milton Meltzer
Black Magic
Englewood Cliffs, N.J.: Prentice-Hall, 1967

Hughes, Laurence A. (ed.)
The Truth about the Movies by the Stars
Hollywood: Hollywood Pubs., 1924

Hughes, Robert (ed.)
Film Book 1: The Audience and the Filmmaker
N.Y.: Grove, 1959

Hughes, Robert (ed.)
Film Book 2: Films of Peace and War
N.Y.: Grove, 1962

Hulfish, David S.
Motion-Picture Work
N.Y.: Arno, 1970 (rp.)

Hunter, William
Scrutiny of Cinema
N.Y.: Arno, 1971 (rp.)

Hurley, Neil P.
Theology through Film
N.Y.: Harper & Row, 1970

Huss, Roy and Norman Silverstein
The Film Experience: Elements of Motion Picture Art
N.Y.: Dell Pub. Co., 1968

Irwin, William H.
The House that Shadows Built
N.Y.: Arno, 1970 (rp.)

Jackson, B. F., Jr. (ed.)
Television-Radio-Film for Churchmen
Nashville, Tenn.: Abingdon Press, 1969

Jacobs, Lewis (ed.)
The Emergence of the Film Art
N.Y.: Hopkinson & Blake, 1969

Jacobs, Lewis (ed.)
Introduction to the Art of the Movies
N.Y.: Noonday, 1960

Jacobs, Lewis (ed.)
The Movies as Medium
N.Y.: Noonday, 1970

Jacobs, Lewis (ed.)
The Rise of the American Film: A Critical History
N.Y.: Columbia Teachers College Press, 1968

Jarvie, I. C.
Movies and Society
N.Y.: Basic Bks., 1970

Jinks, W.
Celluloid Literature: Film in the Humanities
N. Y.: Glencoe Press, 1971

Jobes, Gertrude
Motion Picture Empire
Hamden, Conn.: Archon Bks., 1966

Johnston, Alva
The Great Goldwyn
N. Y.: Random House, 1937

Jones, Bernard E. (ed.)
The Cinematograph Book
London: Casseld & Co., 1915

Jones, Emily
Manual on Film Evaluation
N. Y.: Educational Film Lib. Assn., 1967

Jones, G. Williams
Sunday Night at the Movies
Richmond, Va.: John Knox Press, 1968

Jongbloed, H. J. L. (ed.)
Film Production by International Co-operation
Paris: UNESCO, 1961

Kael, Pauline
Going Steady
Boston: Little, Brown, 1970

Kael, Pauline
I Lost It at the Movies
N. Y.: Bantam Bks., 1965

Kael, Pauline
Kiss Kiss Bang Bang
N. Y.: Bantam Bks., 1969

Kahn, Gordon
Hollywood on Trial
N. Y.: Boni & Gaer, 1948

Kantor, Bernard, Irwin R. Blacker and Ann Kramer
Directors at Work: Interviews with American Film Makers
N. Y.: Funk & Wagnalls, 1970

Kardish, L.
Reel Plastic Magic: A History of Films & Filmmaking in America
Boston: Little, Brown, 1971

Kauffmann, Stanley
Figures of Light: Film Criticism and Comment
N. Y.: Harper & Row, 1971

Kauffman, Stanley
A World on Film: Criticism and Comment
N. Y.: Delta Bks., 1966

Keliher, Alice V. (ed.)
Movie Workers
N. Y.: Harper & Bros., 1939

Kennedy, Donald
So You Think You Know Movies
N. Y.: Ace, 1970

Kennedy, Joseph P.
The Story of the Films as Told by Leaders of the Industry
N. Y.: Jerome S. Ozer, 1971 (rp.)

Kepes, Gyorgy (ed.)
The Nature and Art of Motion
N. Y.: George Braziller, 1965

Kerr, Walter
Criticism and Censorship
Milwaukee, Wisc.: Bruce Pub.
 Co., 1954

Kiesling, Barrett C.
Talking Pictures
Richmond, N.Y.: Johnson Pub.
 Co., 1937

Kirschner, A. and L. Kirschner
 (eds.)
Film: Readings in the Mass Media
N.Y.: Bobbs-Merrill, 1971

Kirstein, Lincoln, Jay Leyda,
 Mary Losey, et al
Films: A Quarterly of Discussion and Analysis, Nos. 1-4
N.Y.: Arno, 1970 (rp.)

Kitses, Jim
Horizons West: Studies in Authorship in the Western Film
Bloomington, Ind.: U. of Ind.
 Press, 1969

Knight, Arthur
The Liveliest Art
N.Y.: Mentor Bks., 1957

Knight, Arthur and Hollis Alpert
Playboy's Sex in Cinema 1970
Chicago: HMH Pub. Co., 1971

Knowles, Dorothy
The Censor, the Drama and the
 Film 1900-1934
London: George Allen & Unwin,
 1934

Koenigil, Mark
Movies in Society
N.Y.: Robert Speller & Sons,
 1962

Kracauer, Siegfried
Theory of Film: The Redemption
 of Physical Reality
N.Y.: Oxford U. Press, 1960

Kreuger, Miles
American Musical Film
N.Y.: Dutton, 1970

Krows, Arthur E.
The Talkies
N.Y.: H. Holt, 1930

Kuhns, William
Mobile Image: Movies (Media
 Probes Volume 3)
N.Y.: Herder & Herder, 1970

Lahue, Kalton C.
Collecting Classic Films
N.Y.: Hastings House, 1970

Lahue, Kalton C.
Dreams for Sale: The Rise and
 Fall of the Triangle Film Corporation
Cranbury, N.J.: Barnes, 1971

Lahue, Kalton C.
Mack Sennett's Keystone: The
 Man, the Myth and the Comedies
Cranbury, N.J.: Barnes, 1971

Lahue, Kalton C. and Terry
 Brewer
Kops and Custards: The Legend
 of Keystone Films
Norman, Okla.: U. of Okla.
 Press, 1967

Lambert, Richard S. (ed.)
For Filmgoers Only: The Intelligent Filmgoer's Guide to the Film
London: Faber & Faber, 1934

Lane, Tamar
What's Wrong with the Movies?
N.Y.: Jerome S. Ozer, 1971 (rp.)

Langer, Susanne K.
Feeling and Form
N.Y.: C. Scribner's Sons, 1953

Langer, Susanne K.
Philosophy in a New Key
N.Y.: Mentor Bks., 1948

Larson, Rodger and Ellen Meade
Young Filmmakers
N.Y.: Avon, 1971

Lasky, Jesse and Don Weldon
I Blow My Own Horn
Garden City, N.Y.: Doubleday, 1957

Laws, Frederick (ed.)
Made for Millions
London: Contact, 1947

Lawson, John H.
Film in the Battle of Ideas
N.Y.: Masses & Mainstream, 1953

Lawson, John H.
Film: The Creative Process
N.Y.: Hill & Wang, 1964

Lee, Norman
Log of a Film Director
London: Quality Press, 1949

Legg, Stuart and R. Fairthorne
The Cinema and Television
London: Longmans, Green, 1939

Le Harivel, Jean P.
Focus on Films
London: C.A. Watts, 1952

Lejeune, Caroline A.
Cinema
London: A. Maclehose & Co., 1931

Lennig, Arthur (ed.)
Classics of the Film
Madison, Wisc.: Wisc. Film Society, 1965

Lennig, Arthur (ed.)
Film Notes
Madison, Wisc.: Wisc. Film Society, 1960

Lennig, Arthur
The Silent Voice: A Text
Troy, N.Y.: W. Snyder, 1969

Lescaboura, Austin G.
Behind the Motion Picture Screen
N.Y.: Scientific American Pub. Co., 1919

Lewin, William and Alexander Frazier
Standards of Photoplay Appreciation
N.J.: Educational & Recreational Guides, 1957

Lewis, Howard T.
The Motion Picture Industry
N.Y.: Jerome S. Ozer, 1971 (rp.)

Lewis, Leon and William D. Sherman
Landscape of Contemporary Cinema
Buffalo: Buffalo Spectrum Press, 1967

Leyda, Jay
Films Beget Films
N.Y.: Hill & Wang, 1964

Likeness, George C.
The Oscar People: From Wings to My Fair Lady
Mendota, Ill.: Wayside Press, 1965

Linden, George W.
Reflections on the Screen
Belmont, Cal.: Wadsworth Pub. Co., 1970

Lindgren, Ernest
The Art of the Film
N.Y.: Macmillan, 1962 (rp.)

Lindgren, Ernest
A Picture History of the Cinema
London: Vista Bks., 1960

Lindsay, Vachel
The Art of the Moving Picture
N.Y.: Liveright Pub. Corp., 1970 (rp.)

Livingston, Don
Film and the Director
N.Y.: Macmillan, 1953

Livingston, Don
Film and the Director: A Handbook and Guide to Film Direction
N.Y.: G. P. Putnam's Sons, 1969 (rp.)

London Film Society
Film Society Programmes 1925 to 1936
N.Y.: Arno, (rp.)

London Science Museum (eds.)
First Colour Motion Pictures
N.Y.: British Information Services,

Look, The Editors of
Movie Lot to Beachhead
Garden City, N.Y.: Doubleday, Doran, 1945

Lowe, Thomas A.
We All Go to the Pictures
London: Wm. Hodge, 1937

MacCann, Richard D. (ed.)
Film: A Montage of Theories
N.Y.: Dutton, 1966

MacCann, Richard D. (ed.)
Film and Society
N.Y.: C. Scribner's Sons, 1964

MacCann, Richard D.
Hollywood in Transition
Boston: Houghton Mifflin, 1962

Macdonald, Dwight
Against the American Grain
N.Y.: Vintage Press, 1962

Macdonald, Dwight
Dwight Macdonald on Movies
Englewood Cliffs, N.J.: Prentice-Hall, 1969

Macgowan, Kenneth
Behind the Screen: The History and Techniques of the Motion Picture
N.Y.: Dell Pub. Co., 1967

MacPherson, Kenneth and
  Winifred Bryher
Close Up
N.Y.: Arno, 1970 (rp.)

Maddux, Rachel, Stirling
  Silliphant and Neil D. Isaacs
Fiction into Film: A Walk in the
  Spring Rain
Knoxville, Tenn.: U. of Tenn.
  Press, 1970

Manvell, Roger
Film
N.Y.: Penguin, 1944

Manvell, Roger
The Living Screen
London: G. G. Harrap & Co.,
  1961

Manvell, Roger
New Cinema in the U.S.A.
N.Y.: Dutton, 1966

Manvell, Roger (ed.)
The Penquin Film Review (9 nos.)
Baltimore: Penguin, 1947-1949

Manvell, Roger
A Seat at the Cinema
London: Evans Bros., 1951

Manvell, Roger
Shakespeare and the Film
N.Y.: Praeger, 1971

Manvell, Roger
What Is a Film?
N.Y.: Trident Press, 1965

Marcus, F. H.
Film from Literature: Contrasts
  in Media
San Francisco: Chandler Pubs.,
  1971

Marlowe, Don
The Hollywood That Was
Ft. Worth, Tex.: Branch-Smith,
  1968

Martin, Olga L. J.
Hollywood's Movie Command-
  ments
N.Y.: Arno, 1970 (rp.)

Mast, G.
Short History of the Movies
N.Y.: Pegasus, 1971

Matthews, J. H.
Surrealism and Film
Ann Arbor, Mich.: U. of Mich.
  Press, 1971

Mayer, Arthur
Merely Colossal, the Story of the
  Movies from the Long Chase to
  the Chaise Longue
N.Y.: Simon & Schuster, 1953

Mayer, Jakob P.
Sociology of Film: Studies and
  Documents
N.Y.: Jerome S. Ozer, 1971 (rp.)

Mayer, Michael F.
Foreign Films on American
  Screens
N.Y.: Arno, 1965

Mayersberg, Paul
Hollywood the Haunted House
N.Y.: Stein & Day, 1967

McAnany, Emile G., S.J., and Robert Williams, S.J.
The Filmviewer's Handbook
Glen Rock, N.J.: Paulist Press, 1965

McBride, James
The Contemporary American Avantgarde Program Notes
N.Y.: Gallery of Modern Art, 1964

McBride, Joseph (ed.)
Persistence of Vision--A Collection of Film Criticism
Madison, Wisc.: Wisc. Film Society, 1964

McCarthy, Mary E.
Hands of Hollywood
Hollywood: Photoplay Research Bureau, 1929

McClure, Arthur F. (ed.)
The Movies: An American Idiom
Cranbury, N.J.: Fairleigh Dickinson U. Press, 1971

McGuire, Jeremiah C.
Cinema and Value Philosophy
N.Y.: Philosophical Lib., 1968

McKowen, Clark and William Sparke
It's Only a Movie
Englewood Cliffs, N.J.: Prentice-Hall, 1971

Messel, Rudolph P.
This Film Business
London: E. Benn, 1928

Meunier-Surcouf, C.
L'Art Cinematographique Nos. 1-8
N.Y.: Arno, 1970 (rp.)

Milne, Peter
Motion Picture Directing
N.Y.: Falk Pub. Co., 1922

Minney, Rubeigh J.
Talking of Films
London: Home & Van Thal, 1947

Moholy-Nagy, Laszlo
The New Vision, and Abstract of an Artist
N.Y.: Wittenborn & Co., 1946

Moholy-Nagy, Laszlo
Painting, Photography, Film
Cambridge, Mass.: MIT Press, 1969

Moholy-Nagy, Laszlo
Vision in Motion
Chicago: Paul Theobald, 1947

Moley, Raymond
The Hays Office
N.Y.: Jerome S. Ozer, 1971 (rp.)

Montagu, Ivor
Film World: A Guide to Cinema
Baltimore: Penquin, 1964

Munro, Thomas
The Arts and Their Interrelations
N.Y.: Liberal Arts Press, 1949

Musical Film
See Category 4: Film Genre

Music for Film
   See Category 2: Film Production and Technology I--Contemporary

Muybridge, Eadweard
Animals in Motion
N.Y.: Dover Pubs., 1957 (rp.)

Muybridge, Eadweard
The Human Figure in Motion
London: Dover Pubs., 1955 (rp.)

Nathan, George J.
The Popular Theatre
N.Y.: Alfred A. Knopf, 1918

Naumburg, Nancy (ed.)
We Make the Movies
N.Y.: W. W. Norton, 1937

The New York Times Film Reviews, 1913-1968 (6 vols.)
N.Y.: Arno,

Nicoll, Allardyce
Film and Theatre
N.Y.: Thomas Y. Crowell, 1936

Nilsen, Vladimir
The Cinema as a Graphic Art
N.Y.: Hill & Wang, 1959 (rp.)

Niver, Kemp R.
The First Twenty Years, a Segment of Film History
L.A.: Historical Films,

Niver, Kemp R.
In the Beginning: Program Notes to Accompany One Hundred Early Motion Pictures
N.Y.: Brandon Bks., 1967

Noble, Peter
The Negro in Films
N.Y.: Arno, 1970 (rp.)

Noble, Peter (ed.)
Picture Parade
London: Burke Pub. Co., 1949

Noble, Peter
Screen Quiz: 500 Questions and Answers on British and Hollywood Films
London: Pendulum Pubs., 1947

Null, G.
Black Hollywood: The Negro in Motion Pictures
N.Y.: Citadel, 1971

O'Dell, Paul
Griffith and the Rise of Hollywood
Cranbury, N.J.: Barnes, 1970

O'Laoghaire, Liam
Invitation to the Film
Tralee, Ireland: Kerryman, 1946

O'Leary, Liam
The Silent Cinema
N.Y.: Dutton, 1965

O'Leary, Michael G. (ed.)
Dramatic Arts and the Modern Mind
Detroit: Sacred Heart Seminary, 1964

Origins of the Motion Picture
N.Y.: British Information Services,

Orrom, Michael and Raymond Williams
Preface to Film
London: Film Drama, 1954

Osborne, Robert A.
Academy Awards Illustrated
LaHabra, Cal.: E. E. Schworck, 1970

Osborne, Robert A.
Academy Awards Illustrated: A Complete History of Hollywood's Academy Awards in Words and Pictures
Hollywood: Marvin Miller Enterprises, 1965

Osborne, Robert A.
Academy Awards: The Best Pictures
LaHabra, Cal.: ESE Cal., 1971

Osborne, Robert A.
Best Actor: Academy Awards
LaHabra, Cal.: E. E. Schworck, 1970

Osborne, Robert A.
Best Actress: Academy Awards
LaHabra, Cal.: E. E. Schworck, 1970

Osborne, Robert A.
Forty Years with Oscar at the Academy Awards
LaHabra, Cal.: E. E. Schworck, 1970

Paine, Stephen W.
The Christian and the Movies
Grand Rapids, Mich.: Eerdman's, 1957

Palmer, Edwin O.
History of Hollywood
Hollywood, Cal.: A. H. Cawston, 1937

Pechter, Willaim S.
Twenty-four Times a Second: Film and Film Makers
N. Y.: Harper & Row, 1970

Percy, Walker
Moviegoer
N. Y.: Noonday, 1961

Perelman, Sidney J.
Crazy Like a Fox
N. Y.: Random House, 1944

Perry, Edward S.
A Contextual Study of Michelangelo Antonioni's Film, L'Eclisse
Iowa City, Ia.: U. of Ia., 1968

Phillips, Henry A.
The Photodrama
N. Y.: Arno, 1970 (rp.)

Photography (motion picture)
See Category 2: Film Production and Technology I--Contemporary

Popescu Gopo, Ion
All about Films
Bucharest: Meridiane Pub. House, 1963

Powell, Pilys
Films Since 1939
London: Longmans, Green, 1947

Pratt, George C. (ed.)
Spellbound in Darkness: Readings in the History and Criticism of the Silent Film (2 vols.)
Rochester, N.Y.: U. of Rochester, 1966

Price, Ira
A Hundred Million Movie-Goers Must Be Right: An Aid to Movie Appreciation
Cleveland: Movie Appreciation Press, 1938

Pryor, William C. and Helen Sloman Pryor
Let's Go to the Movies
N.Y.: Harcourt, Brace & Co., 1939

Pudovkin, V. I.
Film Technique and Film Acting
N.Y.: Grove, 1960

Quigley, Martin, Jr.
Magic Shadows, the Story of the Origin of Motion Pictures
N.Y.: Quigley Pub. Co., 1960

Quigley, Martin, Jr. (ed.)
New Screen Techniques
N.Y.: Quigley Pub. Co., 1953

Quigley, Martin and Richard Gertner
Films in America
Racine, Wisc.: Golden Press, 1970

Quinn, James
Film and Television as an Aspect of European Culture
N.Y.: Humanities Press, 1969

Ramsaye, Terry
A Million and One Nights: A History of the Motion Picture through 1925
N.Y.: Simon & Schuster, 1964 (rp.)

Rathbun, John B.
Motion Picture Making and Exhibiting
Chicago, Ill.: Charles C. Thompson, 1914

Reed, Rex
Big Screen, Little Screen
N.Y.: Macmillan, 1970

Reed, Rex
Conversations in the Raw: Dialogues, Monologues and Selected Short Subjects
Cleveland: World Pub. Co., 1969

Reed, Rex
Do You Sleep in the Nude?
N.Y.: Signet Bks., 1968

Reed, Stanley
The Cinema
London: Educational Supply Assn., 1959

Reed, Stanley
A Guide to Good Viewing
London: Educational Supply Assn., 1961

Reed, Stanley and John Huntley
How Films Are Made
London: Educational Supply Assn., 1959

Reille, Louis
Films in Focus
Meinrad, Ind.: Abbey Press, 1970

Renan, Sheldon
An Introduction to the American Underground Film
N.Y.: Dutton, 1967

Reyertson, A. J.
The Work of the Film Director
N.Y.: Hastings House, 1970

Rhode, Eric
Tower of Babel: Speculations on the Cinema
Philadelphia: Chilton, 1966

Richardson, Robert
Literature and Film
Bloomington, Ind.: Ind. U. Press, 1969

Riddle, Melvin
Pen to Silversheet
L.A.: Harvey White, 1922

Rideout, Eric
The American Film
London: Mitre Press, 1957

Rivkin, Allen and Laura Kerr
Doubleday & Co., Inc., Presents the Rivkin-Kerr Production of Hello Hollywood! A Book about the Movies by the People Who Make Them
N.Y.: Doubleday, 1962

Robinson, David
Hollywood in the Twenties
N.Y.: Barnes, 1968

Robinson, William R. and George Jarrett (eds.)
Man and the Movies: Essays on the Art of Our Time
Baton Rouge, La.: La. Ste. U. Press, 1967

Robson, E. W. and M. M. Robson
The Film Answers Back
London: John Lane, 1939

Robson, E. W. and M. M. Robson
The World Is My Cinema
London: Sidneyan Society, 1947

Rosenbaum, J. (ed.)
Film Masters: An Anthology of Criticism on Thirty-two Film Directors
N.Y.: Grosset & Dunlap, 1971

Rosenberg, Bernard and Harry Silverstein
Real Tinsel: The Story of Hollywood Told by the Men and Women Who Lived It
N.Y.: Macmillan, 1970

Rosenthal, George S.
Life and Death in Hollywood
Cincinnati: Zebra Picture Bks., 1950

Ross, Lillian and Helen Ross
The Player: A Profile of an Art
N.Y.: Simon & Schuster, 1962

Ross, Theodore J.
Film and the Liberal Arts
N.Y.: Holt, Rinehart & Winston, 1970

Rosten, Leo C.
Hollywood: The Movie Colony and the Movie Makers
N.Y.: Arno, 1970 (rp.)

Rotha, Paul
Celluloid: The Film To-Day
London: Longmans, Green, 1931

Rotha, Paul
Movie Parade
N.Y.: Studio Pubs., 1950

Rotha, Paul
Rotha on the Film
London: Faber & Faber, 1958

Rotha, Paul and Richard Griffith
The Film Till Now: A Survey of World Cinema
N.Y.: Twayne Pubs., 1960

Samuels, Charles T.
A Casebook on Film
N.Y.: Van Nostrand Reinhold, 1970

Sarris, Andrew
The American Cinema: Directors and Directions 1929-68
N.Y.: Dutton, 1968

Sarris, Andrew
Confessions of a Cultist: On the Cinema-1955/1969
N.Y.: Simon & Schuster, 1970

Sarris, Andrew
The Film
Indianapolis: Bobbs-Merrill, 1968

Sarris, Andrew
Interviews with Film Directors
Indianapolis: Bobbs-Merrill, 1967

Savary, L. M. et al
Contemporary Film and the New Generation
N.Y.: Assn. Press, 1971

Scheuer, Steven and John Culkin, S. J.
How to Study a Movie: An Introductory Guide to the Art of Motion Pictures
N.Y.: Dell Pub. Co., 1969

Schickel, Richard
The Disney Version
N.Y.: Avon, 1968

Schickel, Richard
Movies: The History of an Art and an Institution
N.Y.: Basic Bks., 1964

Science Fiction Films
  See Category 4: Film Genre

Screen Monographs I
N.Y.: Arno, 1970 (rp.)
Includes:
    Faure, Èlie, The Art of Cineplastics
    Gordon, Bernard and Julian Zimet, The Technique of the Film
    White, Eric W., Parnassus to Let

Screen Monographs II
N.Y.: Arno, 1970 (rp.)
Includes:
    Fletcher, John G., The Crisis of the Film
    Hannon, William M., The Photodrama
    Hays, Will H., See and Hear
    Soupault, Philippe, The American Influence in France

Seabury, William M.
The Public and the Motion Picture Industry
N.Y.: Jerome S. Ozer, 1971 (rp.)

Seldes, Gilbert V.
The Great Audience
N.Y.: Viking, 1950

Seldes, Gilbert V.
An Hour with the Movies and the Talkies
Philadelphia: Lippincott, 1929

Seldes, Gilbert V.
The Movies Come from America
N.Y.: C. Scribner's Sons, 1937

Seldes, Gilbert V.
Movies for the Millions: An Account of Motion Pictures, Principally in America
London: B. T. Batsford, 1937

Seldes, Gilbert V.
The Public Arts
N.Y.: Simon & Schuster, 1956

Seldes, Gilbert V.
The Seven Lively Arts
N.Y.: Sagamore Press, 1957

Sennett, T.
Warner Brothers Presents
New Rochelle, N.Y.: Arlington House, 1971

Serials, Film
See Category 4: Film Genre

Seton, Marie
Film Appreciation: The Art of Five Directors
New Delhi: National Institute of Audio Visual Education, 196?

Sheehan, Perley P.
Hollywood as a World Center
Hollywood: Hollywood Citizen Press, 1924

Sherwood, Robert (ed.)
The Best Moving Pictures of 1922-1923
Boston: Small, Maynard, 1923

Simon, John
Acid Test
N.Y.: Stein & Day, 1963

Simon, John
Movies into Films: Film Criticism 1967-1970
N.Y.: Dial Press, 1971

Simon, John
Private Screenings
N.Y.: Macmillan, 1967

Sitney, P. Adams
Film Culture Reader
N.Y.: Praeger, 1970

Slide, Anthony
Early American Cinema
N.Y.: Barnes, 1970

Smith, Albert E. and P. A. Koury
Two Reels and a Crank
N.Y.: Doubleday, 1952

Sound for Motion Pictures
See Category 2: Film Production and Technology I--Contemporary

Soupault, Philippe
The American Influence in France
Reissued in Screen Monographs II. N.Y.: Arno, 1970

Spatz, Jonas
Hollywood in Fiction: Some Versions of the American Myth
N.Y.: Humanities Press, 1970

Spears, Jack
Hollywood: The Golden Era
Cranbury, N.J.: Barnes, 1970

Spencer, D.A. and H.D. Waley
The Cinema To-Day
N.Y.: Oxford U. Press, 1956

Spottiswoode, Raymond
A Grammar of the Film
Berkeley: U. of Cal. Press, 1962 (rp.)

Starr, Cecile (ed.)
Film Society Primer: A Compilation of Twenty-two Articles about and for Film Societies
Forest Hills, N.Y.: American Federation of Film Societies, 1956

Stauffacher, Frank (ed.)
Art in Cinema
N.Y.: Arno, 1970 (rp.)

Stephenson, Ralph and Jean R. Debrix
The Cinema as Art
Baltimore: Penguin, 1969 (rev. ed.)

Stonier, George W.
Gog, Magog, and Other Critical Essays
London: Dent, 1933

Summers, Stanford
Secular Films and the Church's Ministry
N.Y.: Seabury Press,

Svitak, Ivan
Film in a Manipulated World
N.Y.: Atheneum Pubs., 1970

Talbot, Daniel (ed.)
Film: An Anthology
Berkeley: U. of Cal. Press, 1966

Talbot, Frederick A.
Moving Pictures, How They Are Made and Worked
N.Y.: Arno, 1970 (rp.)

Taylor, Cora W. (comp.)
Masters and Masterpieces of the Screen
N.Y.: P.F. Collier & Son, 1927

Taylor, Deems
A Pictorial History of the Movies
N.Y.: Simon & Schuster, 1950

Thomas, Bob
King Cohn
N.Y.: G.P. Putnam's Sons, 1967

Thomas, Bob
Thalberg: Life and Legend
Garden City, N.Y.: Doubleday, 1969

Thomson, David
Movie Man
N.Y.: Stein & Day, 1967

Thorp, Margaret F.
America at the Movies
N.Y.: Arno, 1970 (rp.)

Thrasher, Frederic (ed.)
Okay for Sound... How the Screen Found Its Voice
N.Y.: Duell, Sloan & Pearce, 1946

Towers, Harry A. and Leslie Mitchell
The March of the Movies
London: S. Low Marston, 1947

Tyler, Parker
Classics of the Foreign Film
N.Y.: Citadel, 1962

Tyler, Parker
The Hollywood Hallucination
N.Y.: Creative Age Press, 1944

Tyler, Parker
Magic and Myth of the Movies
N.Y.: H. Holt, 1947

Tyler, Parker
The Three Faces of the Film: The Art, the Dream and the Cult
N.Y.: Yoseloff, 1960

Tyler, Parker
Underground Film: A Critical History
N.Y.: Grove, 1969

Underground Film
    Also see Category 4: Film Genre

Vance, M. F.
Movie Quiz Book
N.Y.: Paperback Lib., 1970

Van Zile, Edward S.
That Marvel, the Movie
N.Y.: G. P. Putnam's Sons, 1923

Vardac, A. Nicholas
Stage to Screen
N.Y.: Benjamin Blom, 1968 (rp.)

Vereker, Barbara
The Story of Films
London: Hutchinson, 1961

Vidor, King
A Tree Is a Tree
N.Y.: Harcourt, Brace & Winston, 1953

Vizzard, Jack
See No Evil: Life inside a Hollywood Censor
N.Y.: Simon & Schuster, 1970

Wagenknecht, Edward
The Movies in the Age of Innocence
Norman, Okla.: U. of Okla., 1962

Waldekranz, Rune
Modern Film
Stockholm: Wahlström & Widstrand, 1951

War Films
    See Category 4: Film Genre

Warner, Jack L.
My First Hundred Years in Hollywood
N.Y.: Random House, 1964

Warren, Low
The Film Game
London: T. W. Laurie, 1937

Warshow, Robert
The Immediate Experience: Movies, Comics, Theatre and Other Aspects of Popular Culture
Garden City, N.Y.: Doubleday, 1962

Watts, Stephen (ed.)
Behind the Screen: How Films Are Made
London: A. Barker, 1938

Weinberg, Herman G.
Saint Cinema
N.Y.: DBS Pubs., 1970

West, Jessamyn
To See the Dream
N.Y.: Harcourt, Brace & World, 1957

Westerns
See Category 4: Film Genre

Whitaker, Rod
The Language of Film
Englewood Cliffs, N.J.: Prentice-Hall, 1970

White, David M. and Richard Averson
Sight, Sound, and Society: Motion Pictures and Television in America
Boston: Beacon, 1968

Wilk, Max
Wit and Wisdom of Hollywood: From the Squaw Man to Hatchet Man
N.Y.: Atheneum Pubs., 1970

Williams, Raymond and Michael Orrom
Preface to Film
London: Film Drama, 1954

Winnington, Richard
Drawn and Quartered: A Selection of Weekly Film Reviews and Drawings
London: Saturn Press, 1949

Wiseman, Thomas
Cinema
London: Cassell, 1964

Wiseman, Thomas
The Seven Deadly Sins of Hollywood
London: Oldbourne Press, 1957

Wollen, Peter
Signs and Meaning in the Cinema
Bloomington, Ind.: Ind. U. Press, 1969

Wollen, Peter (ed.)
Working Papers on the Cinema: Sociology and Semiology
London: British Film Inst., 1969

Wollenberg, Hans H.
Anatomy of the Film: An Illustrated Guide to Film Appreciation Based on a Course of Cambridge University Extension Lectures
London: Marsland Pubs., 1947

Wood, Leslie
The Miracle of the Movies
London: Burke, 1947

Wood, Michael
The Fabulous Films of the Twenties
N.Y.: Archer House, 1960

Woodhouse, Bruce
From Script to Screen
London: Winchester Pubs., 1948

Wright, Edward A.
A Primer for Playgoers: An Introduction to the Understanding and Appreciation of Cinema, Stage, Television
Englewood Cliffs, N. J.: Prentice-Hall, 1958

Wrigley, M. Jackson and Eric Leyland
The Cinema; Historical, Technical, and Bibliographical: A Survey for Librarians and Students
London: Grafton & Co., 1939

Writing for Film
See Category 2: Film Production and Technology I--Contemporary

Young, Vernon
Cinema Borealis
N. Y.: David Lewis, 1970

Youngblood, Gene
Expanded Cinema
N. Y.: Dutton, 1970

Yurka, Blanche
Dear Audience
Englewood Cliffs, N. J.: Prentice-Hall, 1959

Zinman, David H.
50 Classic Motion Pictures: The Stuff That Dreams Are Made of
N. Y.: Crown, 1970

Zinsser, William K.
Seen Any Good Movies Lately?
Garden City, N. Y.: Doubleday, 1958

Zukor, Adolph and Dale Kramer
The Public Is Never Wrong
N. Y.: G. P. Putnam's Sons, 1953

CATEGORY 2: FILM PRODUCTION AND TECHNOLOGY I-- CONTEMPORARY

Abramson, Albert
Electronic Motion Pictures
Berkeley: U. of Cal. Press, 1957

Albertson, Lillian
Motion Picture Acting
N. Y.: Funk & Wagnalls, 1947

Alder, R. H.
Movie Making for Everyone
London: Fountain Press, 1960

Aloi, Roberto
Architecture for the Theatre
N. Y.: Wm. S. Heinman, 1958

Alton, John
Painting with Light
N. Y.: Macmillan, 1949

Ankersmit, K. S.
Beginner's Guide to Cine-Photography
N. Y.: McBride Bks., 1962

Atkins, Jim and L. Willette
Filming TV News and Documentaries
Philadelphia: Chilton, 1965

Baddeley, Hugh
How to Edit Amateur Films
N. Y.: Focal Press, 1951

Baddeley, W. Hugh
The Technique of Documentary Film Production
N. Y.: Hastings House, 1963

Bare, Richard L.
The Film Director
N. Y.: Macmillan, 1971

Barton, C. H.
How to Animate Cut-outs for Amateur Films
London: Focal Press, 1960

Bateman, Robert
Hints for the Movie Maker
Hastings-on-Hudson, N. Y.: Morgan & Morgan,

Bateman, Robert
Ideas for Amateur Movies
Hastings-on-Hudson, N. Y.: Morgan & Morgan, 1964

Bateman, Robert
Movie-making as a Pastime
London: Souvenir Press, 1960

Battison, John H.
Movies for TV
N. Y.: Macmillan, 1953

Beranger, Clara
Writing for the Screen
Dubuque, Ia.: W. C. Brown, 1950

Blacker, I. R.
Film Script
L. A.: Nash Pub. Co., 1971

Blair, Preston
Animation
Tustin, Cal.: Walter T. Foster, 1949

Bobker, Lee R.
Elements of Film
N. Y.: Harcourt, Brace & World, 1969

Bomback, Edward S.
8mm Movie Making for Pleasure
Hastings-on-Hudson, N. Y.: Morgan & Morgan,

Bomback, Edward S.
Table-tops and Titles in Colour
London: Fountain Press, 1962

Bomback, R. H.
Cine Data Book
London: Fountain Press, 1950

Bomback, R. H. (ed.)
Handbook of Amateur Cinematography
London: Fountain Press, 1953

Bond, Fred
Better Color Movies
San Francisco: Camera Craft Pub. Co., 1948

Branston, Brian
A Film Maker's Guide
N. Y.: Hillary House, 1968

Brodbeck, Emil E.
Handbook of Basic Motion Picture Techniques
N. Y.: American Photographic Bk. Pub. Co., 1969

Brodbeck, Emil E.
Movie and Videotape Special Effects
Philadelphia: Chilton, 1968

Buchanan, Andrew
Film-making from Script to Screen
London: Phoenix House, 1961

Bulleid, H. A. V.
Special Effects in Cinematography
London: Fountain Press, 1954

Burder, John
The Technique of Editing 16mm Films
N. Y.: Hastings House, 1968

Busfield, Roger M., Jr.
The Playwrights' Art: Stage, Radio, Television, Motion Pictures
N. Y.: Harper, 1958

Cameron, James R.
Sound Motion Pictures: Recording and Reproducing, with Chapters on Motion Picture Studio and Film Laboratory Practices
Coral Gables, Fla.: Cameron Pub. Co., 1950

Cameron, James R.
Third Dimension Movies and E-x-p-a-n-d-e-d Screen
Coral Gables, Fla.: Cameron Pub. Co., 1953

Cameron, James R. and Joseph S. Cifre
Cameron's Encyclopedia: Sound Motion Pictures
Coral Gables, Fla.: Cameron Pub. Co., 1959

Cameron, Ken
Sound and the Documentary Film
London: I. Pitman, 1947

Campbell, Russell (ed.)
Photographic Theory for the Motion Picture Camera
Cranbury, N.J.: Barnes,

Campbell, Russell (ed.)
Practical Motion Picture Photography
Cranbury, N.J.: Barnes, 1971

Carlson, Verne and Sylvia Carlson
The 16mm/35mm Professional Cameraman's Handbook
N.Y.: Hastings House,

Carrick, Edward (pseud.)
Art and Design in the British Film
London: Dennis Dobson, 1948

Carrick, Edward (pseud.)
Designing for Moving Pictures
London: Studio Pubs., 1947

Carroll, John S.
Amphoto Lab Handbook
N.Y.: Hastings House,

Chittock, J.
World Dictionary of Stockshot and Film Production Library
Elmsford, N.Y.: Pergamon,

Clairmont, Leonard
The Professional Cine Photographer
Hollywood: Ver Halen Pub. Co., 1956

Clark, Frank P.
Special Effects in Motion Pictures
N.Y.: Society of Motion Picture and Television Engineers, 1966

Clarke, Charles
Professional Cinematography
Hollywood: American Society of Cinematographers, 1964

Clere, L. P.
Photography, Theory and Practice
N.Y.: Pitman, 1957

Cohen, R. S.
Acting Professionally
Palo Alto, Cal.: National Press Bks., 1971

Corbett, D. J.
Motion Picture and Television Image Control and Processing Techniques
N.Y.: Focal Press, 1968

Curran, Charles W.
The Handbook of Motion Picture Technique for Businessmen
N.Y.: Times Square Productions, 1952

Curran, Charles W.
The Handbook of TV and Film Technique: A Non-Technical Production Guide for Executives
N.Y.: Pellegrini & Cudahy, 1953

Curran, Charles W.
Screen Writing and Production Techniques
N.Y.: Hastings House, 1958

Cushman, G. W.
Movie Making in Eighteen Lessons
Philadelphia: Chilton, 1971

Cushman, George W.
Editing Your Color Movies
San Francisco: Camera Craft Pub. Co., 1959

Daborn, John
Cine Titling
Hastings-on-Hudson, N.Y.: Morgan & Morgan,

Davis, Denys
Cine Hints, Tips, and Gadgets
London: Fountain Press, 1952

Densham, D. H.
The Construction of Research Films
N.Y.: Pergamon, 1959

Dewhurst, H.
Introduction to 3-D: Three Dimensional Photography in Motion Pictures
London: Chapman and Hall, 1954

DeWitt, Jack
Producing Industrial Films, from Fade-in to Fade-out
Cranbury, N.J.: Barnes, 1968

Disney, Walt and staff
The Art of Animation
N.Y.: Simon & Schuster, 1959

Dolan, Robert E.
Music in Modern Media
N.Y.: G. Schirmer, 1967

Duckworth, Paul
Experimental and Trick Photography
N.Y.: Universal Photo Bks., 1961

Eisler, Hanns
Composing for the Films
N.Y.: Oxford U. Press, 1947

Evans, Ralph M., W. T. Hanson, Jr., and W. Lyle Brewer
Principles of Color Photography
N.Y.: Wiley, 1953

Ferguson, Robert
How to Make Movies: A Practical Guide to Group Film-Making
N.Y.: Viking, 1969

Fielding, Raymond
The Technique of Special Effects Cinematography
N.Y.: Hastings House, 1965

Fielding, Raymond
A Technological History of Motion Pictures and Television
Berkeley: U. of Cal. Press, 1967

Fletcher, Alan, Colin Forbes and Bob Gill
Graphic Design: Visual Comparisons
N.Y.: Reinhold, 1964

Frayne, John G. and Halley Wolfe
Elements of Sound Recording
N.Y.: John Wiley & Sons, 1949

Gaskill, Arthur L. and
 D. A. Englander
How to Shoot a Movie Story
Hastings-on-Hudson, N.Y.:
 Morgan & Morgan, 1960

Gibson, Brian
Exposing Cine Film
Hastings-on-Hudson, N.Y.:
 Morgan & Morgan,

Gibson, Brian
Lighting for Cine
Hastings-on-Hudson, N.Y.:
 Morgan & Morgan,

Gilmour, Edwyn
Choosing and Using a Cine Camera
Hastings-on-Hudson, N.Y.:
 Morgan & Morgan,

Gilmour, Edwyn
Choosing and Using a Cine Projector
Hastings-on-Hudson, N.Y.:
 Morgan & Morgan,

Gordon, Jay E.
Motion Picture Production for Industry
N.Y.: Macmillan, 1961

Gowland, Peter
How to Take Better Home Movies
N.Y.: Arco Pub. Co., 1957

Grau, Robert
Stage in the Twentieth Century
Bronx, N.Y.: Benjamin Blom,
 (rp.)

Grosset, Phillip
The Complete Book of Amateur Film Making
London: Evans Bros., 1967

Grosset, Phillip
How to Use 8mm
Hastings-on-Hudson, N.Y.:
 Morgan & Morgan, 1959

Grosset, Phillip
Making 8mm Movies
Hastings-on-Hudson, N.Y.:
 Morgan & Morgan, 1959

Grosset, Phillip
Planning and Scripting Amateur Movies
Hastings-on-Hudson, N.Y.:
 Morgan & Morgan, 1963

Halas, John and Roger Manvell
Design in Motion
N.Y.: Hastings House, 1962

Halas, John and Roger Manvell
The Technique of Film Animation
N.Y.: Focal Press, 1968

Halas, John and Bob Privett
How to Cartoon
N.Y.: Focal Press, 1958

Hall, Ben M.
The Best Remaining Seats: The Story of the Golden Age of the Movie Palace
N.Y.: Bramhall House, 1961

Hall, Nelson
Stage Tricks and Hollywood Exercises: How to Develop Skill in Suppleness and Acrobatics
N.Y.: Exposition Press, 1957

Helfman, Harry
Making Pictures Move
N.Y.: Wm. Morrow, 1969

Helfman, Harry
Making Your Own Movies
San Diego, Cal.: Morrow Pubs., 1970

Herdeg, Walter and John Halas
Film and TV Graphics
N.Y.: Hastings House, 1967

Herman, Lewis
Educational Films: Writing, Directing and Producing for Classroom, Television and Industry
Cleveland: World Pub. Co., 1965

Herman, Lewis
A Practical Manual of Screen Playwriting for Theatre and Television Films
Cleveland: World Pub. Co., 1963

Hewitt, Michael
Your Complete Guide to Starting Cine
London: Fountain Press, 1965

Hill, Cecil A.
Cine-film Projection: A Practical Manual for Users of All Types of 16mm and Narrow Gauge Film Projectors
London: Fountain Press, 1952

Hodapp, William
Face Your Audience
N.Y.: Hastings House, 1956

Hofmann, Charles
Sounds for Silents
N.Y.: DBS Pubs., 1969

Hoppe, I. Bernard
Basic Motion Picture Technology
N.Y.: Hastings House, 1970

Horn, Donald R.
Scenarios! Scenarios! Scenarios!
Philadelphia: Chilton, 1963

Huntley, John
British Film Music
London: Skelton Robinson, 1947

Huntley, John
British Technicolor Films
London: Skelton Robinson, 1949

Huntley, John and Roger Manvell
The Technique of Film Music
N.Y.: Hastings House, 1957

Ingeborg, Arnim and Tolke Ingeborg
Macro Photo and Cine Methods
N.Y.: Hastings House, 1970

Jenkins, Norman
How to Project Substandard Films
N.Y.: Focal Press, 1949

Kehoe, Vincent J.R.
The Technique of Film and Television Make-up
N.Y.: Hastings House, 1958

Kemp, Jerrold E. and others
Planning and Producing Audio-Visual Material
San Francisco: Chandler Pubs., 1967

Kinsey, Anthony
How to Make Animated Movies
N.Y.: Viking, 1970

Kloepfel, Don V. (ed.)
Motion Picture Projection and Theatre Presentation Manual
N.Y.: Society of Motion Picture & Television Engineers, 1969

Knight, Bob
Making Home Movies
N.Y.: Macmillan, 1965

Kuhns, William and Robert Stanley
Behind the Camera: Filmmaking for Students
Dayton: George A. Plaum, 1970

Larson, Egon (pseud.)
Film Making
London: Frederick Muller, 1962

Larson, Orville K. (ed.)
Scene Design for Stage and Screen
E. Lansing, Mich.: Mich. Ste. U. Press, 1961

Lawson, John H.
Theory and Technique of Playwriting and Screenwriting
N.Y.: G. P. Putnam's Sons, 1949

Levitan, Eli L.
Animation Art in the Commercial Film
N.Y.: Reinhold, 1960

Levitan, Eli L.
Animation Techniques and Commercial Film Production
N.Y.: Van Nostrand Reinhold, 1962

Levy, Louis
Music for the Movies
London: S. Low Marston, 1948

Lewin, Frank
The Sound Track in Non-Theatrical Motion Pictures
N.Y.: Society of Motion Picture & Television Engineers, 1959

Lidstone, John and Don McIntosh
Children as Film Makers
N.Y.: Van Nostrand Reinhold, 1970

Livingston, Don
Film and the Director: A Handbook and Guide to Film Direction
N.Y.: G. P. Putnam's Sons, 1969

London, Kurt
Film Music: A Summary of the Characteristic Features of Its History, Aesthetics and Technique
N.Y.: Arno, 1970 (rp.)

Mankovsky, V. S.
Acoustics of Sound Studios and Auditoria
N.Y.: Hastings House, 1970

Manoogian, Haig P.
The Film-Maker's Art
N.Y.: Basic Bks., 1966

Manvell, Roger
The Animated Film
London: Sylvan Press, 1954

Manvell, Roger and John Huntley
The Techniques of Film Music
London: Focal Press, 1957

Marner, T.
Directing Motion Pictures
Cranbury, N.J.: Barnes, 1971

Mascelli, Joseph V. (ed.)
American Cinematographer Manual
Hollywood: American Society of Cinematographers, 1960

Mascelli, Joseph V.
The Five C's of Cinematography
Hollywood: Cine/Grafic Pubs., 1966

Matzkin, Myron A.
Better Super 8 Movie Making
Philadelphia: Chilton, 1967

Matzkin, Myron A.
8mm and 16mm Movie Equipment Rating Guide
N.Y.: Universal Photo Bks., 1958

Matzkin, Myron A.
Family Movie Fun for All
N.Y.: Grosset & Dunlap,

McCarty, Clifford
Film Composers in America, a Checklist of Their Work
Glendale, Cal.: J. Valentine, 1953

McKay, Herbert C.
Movie Making for the Beginner
N.Y.: Crown, 1953

McKay, Herbert C.
Three Dimensional Photography
N.Y.: American Photography, 1953

Mercer, John
Introduction to Cinematography
Champaign, Ill.: Stipes Pub. Co., 1968

Miller, Arthur C. and Walter Strenge
American Cinematographer Manual
Hollywood: American Society of Cinematographers, 1966

Mitchell, Robert A.
Manual of Practical Projection
N.Y.: International Projectionist Pub. Co., 1956

Monier, Pierre
The Complete Technique of Making Films
N.Y.: Ballantine, 1968

Neale, Denis M.
How to Add Sound to Amateur Films
N.Y.: Focal Press, 1958

Nisbett, Alex
The Technique of the Sound Studio
N.Y.: Hastings House, 1962

Nurnberg, W.
Lighting for Photography
Philadelphia: Chilton, 1968

Offenhauser, W. H.
16mm Sound Motion Pictures
N.Y.: Interscience Pubs., 1949

Olson, Harry F.
Acoustical Engineering
Princeton, N.J.: Van Nostrand, 1957

Parker, Norton
Audiovisual Script Writing
New Brunswick, N.J.: Rutgers U. Press, 1968

Pate, Michael
The Film Actor: Acting for Motion Pictures and Television
S. Brunswick, N.J.: Barnes, 1970

Peil, Paul
How to Make a Dirty Movie
L.A.: Holloway House, 1970

Pereira, Arthur (ed.)
Manual of Narrow-Gauge Cinematography
London: Fountain Press, 1952

Petzold, Paul
All-in-One Movie Book
N.Y.: Hastings House, 1969

Pincus, Edward
A Guide to Filmmaking
N.Y.: New American Lib., 1969

Pittaro, Ernest M.
TV and Film Production Data Book
N.Y.: Morgan & Morgan, 1959

Pollock, Norman
Basic 8mm Movie Reference Guide
Philadelphia: Chilton, 1960

Postlethwaite, Herbert A.
Introduction to Cine
Hastings-on-Hudson, N.Y.: Morgan & Morgan, 1960

Provisor, Henry
8mm/16mm Movie-Making
Philadelphia: Chilton, 1970

Pudovkin, V. I.
Film Technique and Film Acting
N.Y.: Grove, 1960

Quick, J. and T. LaBau
Handbook of Film Production
N.Y.: Macmillan, 1971

Rawlings, F.
How to Choose Music for Amateur Films
London: Focal Press, 1955

Rebel, Enrique J.
Great Cameramen: An Annotated Dictionary
N.Y.: Barnes, 1969

Regnier, George and Myron A. Matzkin
Movie Techniques for the Advanced Amateur: 8 and 16mm from Script to Screen
N.Y.: American Photographic Pub. Co., 1959

Reisz, Karel and Gavin Millar
The Technique of Film Editing
N.Y.: Hastings House, 1967

Reports of the Commissions on Technical Needs in Press, Radio and Film
Paris: UNESCO, 1947-51

Reynertson, A. J.
The Work of the Film Director
N.Y.: Hastings House, 1970

Rider, Richard L.
A Comparative Analysis of Directing Television and Film Drama
Ann Arbor, Mich.: Univ. Microfilms, 1958

Rilla, Wolf
A-Z of Movie Making
N.Y.: Viking, 1970

Roberts, Kenneth H. and Win Sharples, Jr.
A Primer for Film Making
N.Y.: Pegasus, 1970

Rose, Jackson J.
American Cinematographer Handbook and Reference Guide
Hollywood: American Society of Cinematographers, 1947

Rose, Tony
How to Direct as an Amateur
N.Y.: Focal Press, 1958

Rose, Tony
The Simple Art of Making Films
N.Y.: Focal Press, 1957

Rose, Tony
Tackle Movie Making This Way
London: S. Paul, 1960

Ross, Lillian and Helen Ross
The Player: A Profile of an Art
N.Y.: Simon & Schuster, 1962

Ross, Rodger J.
Color Film for Color Television
N.Y.: Hastings House, 1970

Ross, Rodger J.
Television Film Engineering
N.Y.: John Wiley & Sons, 1966

Rudman, Jack
Civil Service Examination Passbook: Film Editor
Brooklyn, N.Y.: National Learning Corp.,

Rudman, Jack
Civil Service Examination Passbook: Motion Picture Operator
Brooklyn, N.Y.: National Learning Corp.,

Salkin, Leo
Make Your Own Movies
N.Y.: Arco Pub. Co., 1959

Salkin, Leo
Story-Telling Home Movies: How to Make Them
N.Y.: McGraw-Hill, 1958

Script Writing for Short Films
Paris: UNESCO, 1969

Sewell, George H.
Making and Showing Your Own Films
London: Newnes, 1954

Sharp, Dennis
The Picture Palace and Other Buildings for the Movies
N.Y.: Praeger, 1969

Sharps, Wallace S.
Dictionary of Cinematography
 and Sound Recording
Hastings-on-Hudson, N. Y.:
 Morgan & Morgan, 1959

Simpson, Margaret
Film Projecting without Tears or
 Technicalities
London: National Committee for
 Audio-Visual Aids in Education,
 1966

Skilbeck, Oswald
ABC of Film and TV Working
 Terms
London: Focal Press, 1960

Skinner, Frank
Underscore
Hackensack, N. J.: Wehman
 Bros.,

Smallman, Kirk
Creative Film-Making
N. Y.: Macmillan, 1969

Souto, H. Mario R.
The Technique of the Motion Picture Camera
N. Y.: Hastings House, 1967

Spooner, Peter
Business Films: How to Make
 and Use Them
N. Y.: International Publications
 Service, 1959

Spottiswoode, Raymond
Film and Its Techniques
Berkeley: U. of Cal. Press, 1951

Spottiswoode, Raymond et al
 (eds.)
The Focal Encyclopedia of Film
 and Television Techniques
N. Y.: Hastings House, 1969

Spottiswoode, Raymond and Nigel
 Spottiswoode
The Theory of Stereoscopic
 Transmission and Its Application to the Motion Picture
Berkeley: U. of Cal. Press, 1953

Spratt, Hector G.
Magnetic Tape Recording
N. Y.: Van Nostrand Reinhold,
 1964

Stote, Helen M. (ed.)
The Motion Picture Theater:
 Planning, Upkeep
N. Y.: Society of Motion Picture
 Engineers, 1948

Thompson, Charles V.
The Film Script
Hastings-on-Hudson, N. Y.:
 Morgan & Morgan, 1962

Townsend, Derek
How to Use 16mm
Hastings-on-Hudson, N. Y.:
 Morgan & Morgan, 1961

Townsend, Derek
The Practical Guide to Holiday
 and Family Movies
London: S. Paul, 1964

Townsend, Derek
Underwater Photography: Movies
 and Still
London: S. Paul, 1964

Vale, Eugene
Technique of Screenplay Writing
N.Y.: Grosset & Dunlap, 1971

Volkmann, Herbert
Film Preservation
London: British Film Inst., 1966

Wain, George
Filming the Family
Hastings-on-Hudson, N.Y.: Morgan & Morgan, 1962

Wallace, Carlton
Cine Photography All the Year Round
London: Evans Bros., 1965

Wallace, Carlton
Cine Photography for Amateurs
London: Evans Bros., 1961

Wallace, Carlton
Making Movies
London: Evans Bros., 1965

Walter, Ernest
The Technique of the Film Cutting Room
N.Y.: Hastings House, 1969

Wheeler, Leslie J.
Phinciples of Cinematography
London: Fountain Press, 1953

Winter, Myrtle and Norman F. Spurr
Film-Making on a Low Budget
Paris: UNESCO, 1960

Worthington, Clifford
The Influence of the Cinema on Contemporary Auditoria Design
London: Pitman, 1952

Wysotsky, Michael Z.
Wide-Screen Cinema and Stereophonic Sound
N.Y.: Hastings House, 1970

Yoakem, Lola G.
TV and Screen Writing
Berkeley: U. of Cal. Press, 1958

Zuckerman, John V.
Music in Motion Pictures: Review of Literature with Implications for Instructional Films
Port Washington, N.Y.: Office of Naval Research, 1949

CATEGORY 3: FILM PRODUCTION AND TECHNOLOGY II-- OF HISTORICAL INTEREST

Abbott, Harold B.
The Complete 9.15 Cinematographer
London: Amateur Photographer and Cinematographer, 1937

Balbi, Charles M.
Talking Pictures and Acoustics
London: Electrical Review, 1931

Ball, Eustace H.
The Art of the Photoplay
N.Y.: Veritas Pub. Co., 1913

Ball, Eustace H.
Photoplay Scenarios
N.Y.: Hearst's International Lib., 1915

Barker, E. F.
The Art of Photoplay Writing
St. Louis, Mo.: Colossus Pub. Co., 1917

Barker, E. F.
Successful Photo-play Writing
N.Y.: Frye Pub. Co., 1914

Bechdolt, Jack
How to Make Your Own Motion Picture Plays
N.Y.: Greenberg, 1926

Bendick, Jeanne and Robert Bendick
Making the Movies
N.Y.: Whittlesey House, 1945

Bennett, Colin N.
The Handbook of Kinematography
London: I. Pitman, 1923

Bernique, Jean (pseud.)
Motion Picture Acting for Professionals and Amateurs
Chicago: Producers Service Co., 1916

Bertsch, Marguerite
How to Write for Moving Pictures
N.Y.: George H. Doran, 1917

Bradley, Willard K.
Inside Secrets of Photoplay Writing
N.Y.: Funk & Wagnalls, 1926

Brown, Bernard
Amateur Talking Pictures and Recording
London: I. Pitman, 1933

Brown, Bernard
Talking Pictures
London: I. Pitman, 1931

Bruce, Robert and Pat Dowling
Camera Secrets of Hollywood
Hollywood: Camera Secrets Pub. Co., 1931

Brunel, Adrian
Filmcraft
London: Newnes, 1935

Brunel, Adrian
Film Production
London: Newnes, 1936

Buchanan, Andrew
The Art of Film Production
London: I. Pitman, 1936

Caine, Clarence J.
How to Write Photo-plays
Philadelphia: D. McKay, 1915

Cameron, James R.
Amateur Movie Craft
Manhattan Beach, N.Y.: Cameron Pub. Co., 1928

Cameron, James R.
Cinematography and Talkies
Woodmont, Conn.: Cameron Pub. Co., 1932

Cameron, James R.
Motion Picture Projection and Sound Pictures
Woodmont, Conn.: Cameron Pub. Co., 1944

Carr, Catherine
The Art of Photoplay Writing
N.Y.: Hannis Jordan, 1914

Carstairs, John P.
Movie Merry-Go-Round
London: Newnes, 1937

Cook, Canfield
Color Movie Making for Everybody
N.Y.: Whittlesey House, 1949

Cook, William W.
Plotto: A New Method of Plot Suggestion for Writers of Creative Fiction
Battle Creek, Mich.: Ellis Pub. Co., 1928

Dangerfield, Fred and Norman Howard
How to Become a Film Artiste: The Art of Photo-Play Acting
London: Odhams Press, 1921

Dench, Ernest A.
Playwriting for the Cinema
London: A. & C. Black, 1914

Dimick, Howard T.
Photoplay Making
Ridgewood, N.J.: Editor Co., 1915

East, Henry R.
How to Train Dogs for the Home, Stage and Moving Pictures
N.Y.: Pitman, 1933

Elliott, W. F.
Sound-Recording for Films
London: I. Pitman, 1937

Emerson, John and Anita Loos
How to Write Photoplays
N.Y.: James A. McCann, 1920

Esenwein, J. Berg and Arthur Leeds
Writing the Photoplay
Springfield, Mass.: Home Correspondence School, 1919

Fanstone, Robert M.
Colour Photography
London: Fountain Press, 1938

Fawcett, L'Estrange
Writing for the Films
London: I. Pitman, 1932

Fox, Charles D.
The Standard Photoplay Plot Chart
Chicago: Fox Photoplay Inst., 1922

Franklin, Harold B.
Sound Motion Pictures
Garden City, N.Y.: Doubleday, Doran, 1929

Gale, Arthur L.
How to Write a Movie
N.Y.: E. B. Hackett, 1936

Gale, Arthur L.
Make Your Own Movies
N.Y.: Coward-McCann, 1939

Gale, Arthur L. and Russell C. Holslag
Making Better Movies
N.Y.: Amateur Cinema League, 1935

Gleason, Marion N.
Scenario Writing and Producing for the Amateur
Boston: American Photographic Co., 1929

Gordon, William L.
How to Write Moving Picture Plays
Cincinnati: Atlas Pub. Co., 1914

Gregory, Carl L. (ed.)
A Condensed Course in Motion Picture Photography
N.Y.: N.Y. Inst. of Photography, 1920

Hacker, Leonard
Cinematic Design
Boston: American Photographic Pub. Co., 1931

Hall, Hal (ed.)
Cinematographic Annual
N.Y.: Arno, 1971 (rp.)

Hepworth, Cecil M.
Animated Photography: The A B C of the Cinematograph
N.Y.: Arno, 1970 (rp.)

Hoagland, Herbert C.
How to Write a Photoplay
N.Y.: Magazine Maker Pub. Co., 1912

Jackson, Arrar
Writing for the Screen
London: A. & C. Black, 1929

Johnson, R. V.
Modern Picture Theatre Electrical Equipment and Projection
London: C. Lockwood & Son, 1925

Jones, G. F.
Sound-Film Reproduction
London: Blackie & Son, 1931

Kelly, Edgar J.
Acting for Pictures: How It's Done and How to Do It
New Orleans: Conte & Frichter Pub. Co., 1916

Kendall, G. P.
Film Titling
London: Newnes, 1935

Klumph, Inea and Helen Klumph
Screen Acting
N.Y.: Falk Pub. Co., 1922

Lane, Tamar
The New Technique of Screen
 Writing, a Practical Guide to
 the Writing and Marketing of
 Photoplays
N.Y.: McGraw-Hill, 1936

Lang, Edith and George West
Musical Accompaniment of Mov-
 ing Pictures
N.Y.: Arno, 1970 (rp.)

Lipton, Lew
Ideas
N.Y.: Chatham Pub. Co., 1937

Lutz, Edwin G.
The Motion Picture Cameraman
N.Y.: Arno, 1971 (rp.)

Lytton, Grace
Scenario Writing Today
N.Y.: Houghton Mifflin, 1921

Macbean, L. C.
Kinematograph Studio Technique
London: I. Pitman & Sons, 1922

Marey, E. J.
Movement
N.Y.: Arno, 1971 (rp.)

Margrave, Seton
Successful Film Writing
London: Methuen & Co., 1936

Marion, Frances
How to Write and Sell Film Sto-
 ries
N.Y.: Covici Friede, 1937

Marsh, Mae
Screen Acting
L.A.: Photo-Star Pub. Co., 1921

McKay, Herbert C.
Amateur Movie Making
N.Y.: Falk Pub. Co., 1928

McKay, Herbert C.
The Ciné Camera
N.Y.: Falk Pub. Co., 1930

McKay, Herbert C.
Ciné Titling and Editing
N.Y.: Falk Pub. Co., 1932

McKay, Herbert C.
The Handbook of Motion Picture
 Photography
N.Y.: Falk Pub. Co., 1927

McKay, Herbert C.
Motion Picture Photography for
 the Amateur
N.Y.: Falk Pub. Co., 1924

McKay, Herbert C.
The Voice of the Films
N.Y.: Falk Pub. Co., 1930

Meloy, Arthur S.
Theatres and Motion Picture
 Houses
N.Y.: Architects' Supply & Pub.
 Co., 1916

Miehling, Rudolph
Sound Projection
N.Y.: Mancall Pub. Corp., 1929

Milne, Peter
Motion Picture Directing
N.Y.: Falk Pub. Co., 1922

Minter, L. F.
How to Title Amateur Films
N.Y.: Focal Press, 1949

Myerscough-Walker, R.
Stage and Film Decor
London: I. Pitman & Sons, 1940

Nadell, Aaron
Projecting Sound Pictures
N.Y.: McGraw-Hill, 1931

O'Dell, Scott
Representative Photoplays Analyzed
Hollywood: Palmer Inst. of Authorship, 1924

Ottley, D. Charles
Making Home Movies
London: Newnes, 1935

Ottley, D. Charles
Practical Set Structure
London: I. Pitman's Sons, 1935

Palmer, Frederick
Author's Photoplay Manual
Hollywood: Palmer Inst. of Authorship, 1924

Palmer, Frederick
Palmer Plan Handbook--Photoplay Writing Simplified and Explained by Frederick Palmer
L.A.: Palmer Photoplay, 1918

Palmer, Frederick
Technique of the Photoplay
Hollywood: Palmer Inst. of Authorship, 1924

Palmer, Frederick and Eric Howard
Photoplay Plot Encyclopedia
L.A.: Palmer Photoplay, 1920

Parsons, Louella O.
How to Write for the "Movies"
Chicago: A. C. McClurg, 1915

Patterson, Frances T.
Cinema Craftsmanship: A Book for Photoplaywrights
N.Y.: Harcourt, Brace & Howe, 1921

Patterson, Frances T.
Scenario and Screen
N.Y.: Harcourt, Brace & Co., 1928

Peacocke, Leslie T.
Hints on Photoplay Writing
Chicago: Photoplay Pub. Co., 1916

Phillips, Henry A.
The Art of Writing Photoplays
Cincinnati: Writer's Digest, 1922

Phillips, Henry A.
The Feature Photoplay
Springfield, Mass.: Home Correspondence School, 1921

Pitkin, Walter B. and William M. Marston
The Art of Sound Pictures
N.Y.: D. Appleton, 1930

Platt, Agnes E.
Practical Hints on Acting for the Cinema
N.Y.: Dutton, 1923

Rapee, Erno
Encyclopedia of Music for Pictures
N.Y.: Arno, 1970 (rp.)

Rapee, Erno
Motion Picture Moods for Pianists and Organists
N.Y.: Arno, 1970 (rp.)

Read, Oliver
The Recording and Reproduction of Sound
Indianapolis: H.W. Sams, 1952

Richardson, Frank H.
Motion Picture Handbook: A Guide for Managers and Operators of Motion Picture Theatres
N.Y.: Moving Picture World, 1910

Robinson, Martha
Continuity Girl
London: R. Hale & Co., 1937

Rysking, Morrie, C. F. Stevens and James Englander
The Home Movie Scenario Book
N.Y.: Richard Manson, 1927

Sabaneev, Leonid
Music for the Films
London: Pitman, 1935

Salzman, Maurice
Plagiarism, the "Art" of Stealing Literary Material
L.A.: Parker, Stone & Baird, 1931

Sargent, Epes W.
The Technique of the Photoplay
N.Y.: Moving Picture World, 1916

Sewell, George H.
Amateur Film-Making
London: Blackie & Son, 1938

Sewell, George H.
Commercial Cinematography
London: I. Pitman & Sons, 1933

Sewell, George H.
Film-play Production for Amateurs
London: Pitman & Sons, 1932

Shand, P. Morton
Motion Picture Houses and Theatres
Philadelphia: Lippincott, 1930

Simon, S. Sylvan
Let's Make Movies
N.Y.: S. French, 1940

Sloane, T. O'Conor
Motion Picture Projection
N.Y.: Falk Pub. Co., 1922

Strasser, Alex
Amateur Films
London: Link House Pubs., 1936

Strasser, Alex
Amateur Movies and How to Make Them
N.Y.: Studio Pubs., 1937

Strasser, Alex
Ideas for Short Films
London: Link House Pubs., 1937

Talbot, Frederick A.
Practical Cinematography and
 Its Applications
London: W. Heinemann, 1913

Thomas, A. W.
How to Write a Photoplay
Chicago: Photoplaywrights'
 Assn. of America, 1914

Welsh, Robert E.
A-B-C of Motion Pictures
N.Y.: Harper & Bros., 1916

Wheeler, Owen
Amateur Cinematography
London: I. Pitman & Sons, 1929

Wheeler, Owen
Colour Photography
London: I. Pitman & Sons, 1928

Wright, William L.
Photoplay Writing
N.Y.: Falk Pub. Co., 1922

CATEGORY 4: FILM GENRE

Atkins, Jim and L. Willette
Filming TV News and Documentaries
Philadelphia: Chilton, 1965

Baddeley, W. Hugh
The Technique of Documentary Film Production
N.Y.: Hastings House, 1963

Baechlin, Peter and Maurice Muller-Strauss
Newsreels across the World
Paris: UNESCO, 1952

Balshofer, Fred J. and Arthur C. Miller
One Reel a Week
Berkeley: U. of Cal. Press, 1967

Barbour, Alan G.
Days of Thrills and Adventure
N.Y.: Macmillan, 1970

Barbour, Alan G. (comp.)
Great Serial Ads
Kew Gardens, N.Y.: Screen Facts Press, 1965

Barbour, Alan G. (comp.)
Serial Showcase
Kew Gardens, N.Y.: Screen Facts Press, 1968

Barbour, Alan G.
The Serials of Republic
Kew Gardens, N.Y.: Screen Facts Press, 1965

Barbour, Alan G.
Thousand and One Delights
N.Y.: Macmillan, 1971

Barbour, Alan G.
The Thrill of It All
N.Y.: Macmillan, 1971

Barbour, Alan G. (comp.)
The Wonderful World of B-Films
Kew Gardens, N.Y.: Screen Facts Press, 1968

Baxter, John
The Gangster Film
Cranbury, N.J.: Barnes, 1970

Baxter, John
Science Fiction in the Cinema
N.Y.: Barnes, 1969

Becker, Stephen
Comic Art in America
N.Y.: Simon & Schuster, 1959

Blistein, Elmer M.
Comedy in Action
Durham, N.C.: Duke U. Press, 1964

Bluem, A. William
Documentary in American Television
N.Y.: Hastings House, 1964

Bluestone, George
Novels into Film
Berkeley: U. of Cal. Press, 1966

Burton, Jack
The Blue Book of Hollywood Musicals: Songs from the Sound Tracks and the Stars Who Sang Them Since the Birth of the Talkies a Quarter-Century Ago
Watkins Glenn, N.Y.: Century House, 1953

Butler, Ivan
The Horror Film
N.Y.: Barnes, 1967

Butler, Ivan
Horror in the Cinema
Cranbury, N.J.: Barnes, 1970

Butler, Ivan
Religion in the Cinema
N.Y.: Barnes, 1969

Cameron, Ken
Sound and the Documentary Film
London: I. Pitman, 1947

Capa, Robert
Images of War
N.Y.: Grossman, 1964

Carson, L. M. Kit
Cinema Verité in America
N.Y.: Museum of Modern Art,

Chertok, Harvey and Martha Torge
Quotations from Charlie Chan
Racine, Wisc.: Western Pub. Co., 1968

Clarens, Carlos
Horror Movies: An Illustrated Survey
London: Secker & Warburg, 1968

Clarens, Carlos
An Illustrated History of the Horror Film
N.Y.: Capricorn Bks., 1967

Curtis, David
Experimental Cinema
N.Y.: Universe Bks., 1970

Documentary and Experimental Films
N.Y.: Museum of Modern Art, 1959

Douglas, Drake (pseud.)
Horror!
N.Y.: Macmillan, 1966

Durgnat, Raymond
The Crazy Mirror: Hollywood Comedy and the American Image
N.Y.: Horizon, 1970

Eastman, Max
Enjoyment of Laughter
N.Y.: Simon & Schuster, 1936

Everson, William K.
A Pictorial History of the Western Film
N.Y.: Citadel, 1969

Eyles, Allen
American Comedy Since Sound
N.Y.: Barnes, 1969

Eyles, Allen
The Western: An Illustrated Guide
N.Y.: Barnes, 1967

Fenin, George N. and William K. Everson
The Western
N.Y.: Orion, 1962

Fernett, Gene
Next Time Drive off the Cliff!
Cocoa, Florida: Cinememories Pubs., 1968

Frantz, Joe B. and J. Choate
The American Cowboy
London: Thames & Hudson, 1956

Gifford, Denis
Movie Monsters
London: Studio Vista, 1969

Gifford, Denis
Science Fiction Film
N.Y.: Dutton, 1971

Gow, Gordon
Suspense in the Cinema
N.Y.: Barnes, 1968

Grierson, John
Grierson on Documentary
Berkeley: U. of Cal. Press, 1966

Halas, John and Roger Manvell
Art in Movement: New Directions in Animation
N.Y.: Hastings House, 1970

Harmon, J. and D. Glut
Movie Serials: Their Sound and Fury
Garden City, N.Y.: Doubleday, 1971

Jenkins, Charles F.
Animated Pictures
N.Y.: Arno, 1970 (rp.)

Knight, Derrick and Vincent Porter
A Long Look at Short Films: An A.C.T.T. Report on the Short Entertainment and Factual Film
N.Y.: Pergamon, 1967

Lahue, Kalton C.
Bound and Gagged
N.Y.: Barnes, 1968

Lahue, Kalton C.
Continued Next Week: A History of the Moving Picture Serial
Norman, Okla.: U. of Okla. Press, 1964

Lahue, Kalton C.
Ladies in Distress
Cranbury, N.J.: Barnes, 1971

Lahue, Kalton C.
Mack Sennett's Keystone: The Man, Myth and the Comedies
Cranbury, N.J.: Barnes, 1971

Lahue, Kalton C.
Winners of the West: The Sagebrush Heroes of the Silent Screen
N.Y.: Barnes, 1970

Lahue, Kalton C.
World of Laughter: The Motion Picture Comedy Short
Norman, Okla.: U. of Okla. Press, 1966

Lahue, Kalton C. and Terry Brewer
Kops and Custards: The Legend of Keystone Films
Norman, Okla.: U. of Okla. Press, 1967

Lahue, Kalton C. and Samuel Gill
Clown Princes and Court Jesters
Cranbury, N.J.: Barnes, 1970

Lee, Ray and Vernell Coriell
A Pictorial History of the Tarzan Movies
L.A.: Golden State News Co., 1966

Lee, Raymond and B. C. Van Hecke
Gangsters and Hoodlums: The Underworld in the Cinema
Cranbury, N.J.: Barnes, 1970

Levin, G. R.
Documentary Explorations: Sixteen Interviews with Film-Makers
Garden City, N.Y.: Doubleday, 1971

Levitan, Eli L.
Animation Art in the Commercial Film
N.Y.: Reinhold Pub. Corp., 1960

Lutz, Edwin G.
Animated Cartoons
N.Y.: C. Scribner's Sons, 1920

Madsen, Roy P.
Animated Film: Concepts, Methods and Uses
N.Y.: Pitman, 1969

Maltin, Leonard
Classical Movie Shorts
N.Y.: Crown, 1971

Manvell, Roger
The Animated Film
London: Sylvan Press, 1954

Manvell, Roger (ed.)
Experiment in the Film
N.Y.: Arno, 1970 (rp.)

McVay, Douglas
The Musical Film
N.Y.: Barnes, 1967

Menville, Douglas A.
A Historical and Critical Survey of the Science-Fiction Film
L.A.: U. of S. Cal. Photographic Service, 1959

Montgomery, John
Comedy Films 1894-1954
London: Allen & Unwin, 1968

Parish, J. R. (ed.)
Great Movie Series
Cranbury, N.J.: Barnes, 1971

Renan, Sheldon
An Introduction to the American Underground Film
N.Y.: Dutton, 1967

Rosenthal, Alan (ed.)
The New Documentary in Action: A Casebook in Film-Making
Berkeley: U. of Cal. Press, 1971

Rotha, Paul, Sinclair Road and Richard Griffith
Documentary Film
N.Y.: Hastings House, 1962

Snyder, Robert L.
Pare Lorentz and the Documentary Film
Norman, Okla.: U. of Okla. Press, 1968

Springer, John
All Talking, All Singing, All Dancing
N.Y.: Citadel, 1966

Starr, Cecile (ed.)
Ideas on Film
N.Y.: Funk & Wagnalls, 1951

Stedman, R.
Serials: Suspense and Drama by Installment
Norman, Okla.: U. of Okla. Press, 1971

Stephenson, Ralph
Animation in the Cinema
N.Y.: Barnes, 1967

Stern, Seymour and Lewis Jacobs (eds.)
Experimental Cinema
N.Y.: Arno, 1970 (rp.)

Taylor, J.R. and A. Jackson
Hollywood Musicals
N.Y.: McGraw-Hill, 1971

Tyler, Parker
Underground Film: A Critical History
N.Y.: Grove, 1969

Vallance, Tom
The American Musical
Cranbury, N.J.: Barnes, 1970

Vallance, Tom
Westerns: A Preview Special
London: Golden Pleasure Bks., 1964

Waldron, Gloria
The Information Film
N.Y.: Columbia U. Press, 1949

Warman, Eric and Tom Vallance
Westerns
London: Golden Pleasure Bks., 1964

Weiss, Ken and Ed Goodgold
To Be Continued
N.Y.: Crown, 1971

Wilde, Larry
The Great Comedians Talk about Comedy
N.Y.: Citadel, 1968

Wright, Basil
The Use of the Film
London: Bodley Head, 1948

CATEGORY 5: SOCIOLOGY AND ECONOMICS OF FILM

Alloway, Lawrence
Violent America: The Movies 1946-1964
N.Y.: Museum of Modern Art, 1971

American Academy of Political and Social Science
The Motion Picture Industry
Philadelphia: American Academy of Political and Social Science, 1947

Bailyn, Lotte
Mass Media and Children: A Study of Exposure Habits and Cognitive Effects
Washington, D.C.: American Psychological Assn., 1959

Barclay, John B.
Viewing Tastes of Adolescents in Cinema and Television
Glasgow: Scottish Educational Film Assn., 1961

Barry, John F. and Epes W. Sargent
Building Theatre Patronage
N.Y.: Chalmers Pub. Co., 1927

Baumol, William J. and William G. Bowen
Performing Arts: The Economic Dilemma
N.Y.: Twentieth Century Fund, 1966

Beckoff, Samuel
An Inquiry into the Operative Principles Applicable to the Licensing of Motion Pictures in New York State
Ann Arbor, Mich.: Univ. Microfilms, 1960

Beman, Lamar T. (comp.)
Selected Articles on Censorship of the Theater and Motion Pictures
N.Y.: Jerome S. Ozer, 1971 (rp.)

Bloom, Samuel W.
A Social Psychological Study of Motion Picture Audience Behavior: A Case Study of the Negro Image in Mass Communication
Ann Arbor, Mich.: Univ. Microfilms, 1956

Blumer, Herbert
Movies and Conduct
N.Y.: Arno, 1970 (rp.)

Blumer, Herbert and Philip M. Hauser
Movies, Delinquency and Crime
N. Y.: Arno, 1970 (rp.)

Bormerl Oaks Press (ed.)
Survey of Rural Taste for T. V. and Movie Stars
Ray, Ind.: Bormerl Oaks Press, 1968

Box, Sydney
Film Publicity
London: L. Dickson, 1937

Boyal, Trishla
The Marketing of Films
Calcutta: Intertrade Pubs., 1966

Brusendorff, Ove and Poul Henningsen
Erotica for the Millions: Love in the Movies
London: Rodney Bk. Service, 1960

Byrne, Richard B.
Films of Tyranny: Shot Analyses of "The Cabinet of Dr. Caligari," "The Golem" and "Nosferatu"
Madison, Wisc.: College Printing and Typing Co., 1966

Carmen, Ira H.
Movies, Censorship and the Law
Ann Arbor, Mich.: U. of Mich. Press, 1966

Cassady, Ralph, Jr., and Ralph Cassady III
The Private Antitrust Suit in American Business Competition: A Motion-Picture Industry Case Analysis
L. A.: U. of Cal., 1964

Charters, W. W.
Motion Pictures and Youth
N. Y.: Arno, 1970 (rp.)

Chittock, John
Film and Effect
London: Financial Times, 1967

Cogley, John
Report on Blacklisting
Ann Arbor, Mich.: Univ. Microfilms, (rp.)

Conant, Michael
Antitrust in the Motion Picture Industry
Berkeley: U. of Cal. Press, 1960

Crowther, Bosley
Movies and Censorship
N. Y.: Public Affairs Pamphlets, 1962

Cunningham, Robert P.
A Sociological Approach to Esthetics: An Analysis of Attitudes toward the Motion Picture
Ann Arbor, Mich.: Univ. Microfilms, 1954

Dale, Edgar
Children's Attendance at Motion Pictures
Issued in one vol. with the following entry:
  Dale, Edgar, Wendell S. Dysinger, and Christian A. Ruckmick
  The Emotional Responses of Children to the Motion Picture Situation
N. Y.: Arno, 1970 (rp.)

Decoulteray, George
Sadism in the Movies
N.Y.: Medical Press, 1965

Dench, Ernest A.
Advertising by Motion Pictures
Cincinnati: Standard Pub. Co., 1916

Durgnat, Raymond
Eros in the Cinema
London: Calder & Boyars, 1966

Ernst, Morris L.
The First Freedom
N.Y.: Macmillan, 1946

Ernst, Morris L. and Pare Lorentz
Censored: The Private Life of the Movies
N.Y.: Jerome S. Ozer, 1971 (rp.)

Ernst, Morris L. and Alan U. Schwartz
Censorship: The Search for the Obscene
N.Y.: Macmillan, 1964

Fagan, Myron C.
Documentation of the Red Stars in Hollywood
Hollywood: Cinema Educational Guild, 1950

Faulk, John H.
Fear on Trial
N.Y.: Simon & Schuster, 1964

Federal Council of the Churches of Christ in America
The Public Relations of the Motion Picture Industry: A Report by the Department of Research and Education
N.Y.: Jerome S. Ozer, 1971 (rp.)

Ford, Richard
Children in the Cinema
N.Y.: Jerome S. Ozer, 1971 (rp.)

Forman, Henry J.
Our Movie Made Children
N.Y.: Arno, 1970 (rp.)

Franklin, Harold B.
Motion Picture Theatre Management
N.Y.: George H. Doran, 1927

Furhammar, L. and F. Isaksson
Politics and Film
N.Y.: Praegar, 1971

Getlein, Frank and Harold C. Gardiner, S.J.
Movies, Morals and Art
N.Y.: Sheed & Ward, 1961

Goode, Kenneth and Zenn Kaufman
Profitable Showmanship
N.Y.: Prentice-Hall, 1939

Grau, Robert
The Business Man in the Amusement World: A Volume of Progress in the Field of the Theatre
N.Y.: Jerome S. Ozer, 1971 (rp.)

Haney, Robert W.
Comstockery in America: Patterns of Censorship and Control
Boston: Beacon, 1960

Harley, John E.
World-Wide Influences of the Cinema: A Study of Official Censorship and the International Cultural Aspects of Motion Pictures
N.Y.: Jerome S. Ozer, 1971 (rp.)

Hendricks, Bill and Howard Waugh
The Encyclopedia of Exploitation
N.Y.: Showmen's Trade Review, 1937

Hills, Janet
Are They Safe at the Cinema?
London: British Film Inst., 1960

Holland, Benjamin F.
Status and Prospects of Film Distribution in Texas
Austin, Tex.: Univ. of Tex. Press, 1958

Huaco, George A.
The Sociology of Film Art
N.Y.: Basic Bks., 1965

Huettig, Mae D.
Economic Control of the Motion Picture Industry: A Study in Industrial Organization
N.Y.: Jerome S. Ozer, 1971 (rp.)

Hughes, Langston and Milton Meltzer
Black Magic
Englewood Cliffs, N.J.: Prentice-Hall, 1967

Hunnings, Neville M.
Film Censors and the Law
N.Y.: Hillary House, 1967

The Influence of the Cinema on Children and Adolescents
Paris: UNESCO, 1961

Inglis, Ruth A.
Freedom of the Movies
Chicago: U. of Chicago, 1947

Ivamy, Edward R. H.
Show Business and the Law
London: Stevens, 1955

Jarvie, I. C.
Movies and Society
N.Y.: Basic Bks., 1970

Jerome, V. J.
The Negro in Hollywood Films
N.Y.: Masses & Mainstream, 1950

Jongbloed, H. J. L. (ed.)
Film Production by International Co-operation
Paris: UNESCO, 1961

Kelly, Terence
Competitive Cinema
N.Y.: International Publications Service, 1966

Klingender, F. D. and S. Legg
Money behind the Screen
London: Lawrence & Wishart, 1937

Knopp, Leslie
The Cinematograph Regulations, 1955
London: Cinema Press, 1956

Knowles, Dorothy
The Censor, the Drama and the Film: 1900-1934
London: George Allen & Unwin, 1934

Koenigil, Mark
Movies in Society
N.Y.: Robert Speller & Sons, 1962

Léglise, Paul
Methods of Encouraging the Production and Distribution of Short Films for Theatrical Use
Paris: UNESCO, 1962

Léglise, Paul
The Theatrical Distribution of Cultural Films
Strasbourg: Council for Cultural Co-operation, Council of Europe, 1967

Legman, Gershon
Love and Death: A Study in Censorship
N.Y.: Hacker Art Bks., 1963

Lloyd, Peter
Not for Publication
London: Bow Publications, 1968

Long, Howard R.
Rural Communication Patterns: A Study in the Availability and Use of Print, Radio and Film in Shelby County, Missouri
Ann Arbor, Mich.: Univ. Microfilms, 1949

Lovell, Hugh and Tasile Carter
Collective Bargaining in the Motion Picture Industry, a Struggle for Stability
Berkeley: U. of Cal., 1955

MacCann, Richard D. (ed.)
Film and Society
N.Y.: C. Scribner's Sons, 1964

Manvell, Roger
The Film and the Public
Baltimore: Penguin, 1955

Marchetti, Roger
Law of the Stage, Screen and Radio
San Francisco: Suttonhouse, 1936

Markun, Leo
Mrs. Grundy: A History of Four Centuries of Morals
N.Y.: D. Appleton, 1930

Mayer, Jakob P.
Sociology of Film: Studies and Documents
N.Y.: Jerome S. Ozer, 1971 (rp.)

McGuire, Jeremiah C.
Cinema and Value Philosophy
N.Y.: Philosophical Lib., 1968

Milner, M.
Sex on Celluloid
N.Y.: Macfadden-Bartell Corp., 1964

Minus, Johnny and William S. Hale (pseuds.)
The Movie Industry Book: How Others Made and Lost Money in the Movie Industry
Hollywood: 7 Arts Press, 1970

Mitchell, Alice M.
Children and Movies
N.Y.: Jerome S. Ozer, 1971 (rp.)

Moley, Raymond
Are We Movie Made?
N.Y.: Macy-Masius, 1938

Moley, Raymond
The Hays Office
N.Y.: Jerome S. Ozer, 1971 (rp.)

Momand, A.B.
Help Wanted, Male and Female: Or The Great Motion Picture Conspiracy, Condensed . . . An Exhibitor's Story . . .
Shawnee, Okla.: Okla. Baptist U. Press, 1949

Motion Picture Producers and Distributors of America
The Community and the Motion Picture: Report of the National Conference on Motion Pictures Held at the Hotel Montclair, New York City, September 24-27, 1929
N.Y.: Jerome S. Ozer, 1971 (rp.)

Munsterberg, Hugo
The Photoplay, a Psychological Study
N.Y.: Dover Pubs., 1969 (rp.)

Murphy, Terrence J.
Censorship: Government and Obscenity
Baltimore: Helicon, 1963

Musun, Chris
The Marketing of Motion Pictures
L.A.: C. Musun, 1969

Nizer, Louis
New Courts of Industry: Self-Regulation under the Motion Picture Code, Including an Analysis of the Code
N.Y.: Jerome S. Ozer, 1971 (rp.)

Noble, Peter
The Negro in Films
N.Y.: Arno, 1970 (rp.)

Null, G.
Black Hollywood: The Negro in Motion Pictures
N.Y.: Citadel, 1971

Oberholtzer, Ellis P.
The Morals of the Movies
N.Y.: Jerome S. Ozer, 1971 (rp.)

Paul, Elliot H.
Film Flam
London: Frederick Muller, 1956

Paul, Elliot H. and Luis Quintanilla
With a Hays Nonny Nonny
N.Y.: Random House, 1942

Perlman, William J. (ed.)
The Movies on Trial: The Views and Opinions of Outstanding Personalities Anent Screen Entertainment Past and Present
N.Y.: Jerome S. Ozer, 1971 (rp.)

Peters, Charles C.
Motion Pictures and Standards of Morality
N.Y.: Arno, 1970 (rp.)

Peterson, Ruth C. and L. I. Thurstone
Motion Pictures and Social Attitudes of Children
N.Y.: Arno, 1970 (rp.)

Pilpel, Harriet F. and Theodora S. Zavin
Rights and Writers: A Handbook of Literary and Entertainment Law
N.Y.: Dutton, 1960

Powdermaker, Hortense
Hollywood, the Dream Factory: An Anthropologist Looks at the Movie-Makers
Boston: Little, Brown, 1950

Quigley, Martin, Jr.
Decency in Motion Pictures
N.Y.: Jerome S. Ozer, 1971 (rp.)

Raborn, George
How Hollywood Rates
Los Altos, Cal.: B. Nelson, 1955

Randall, Richard S.
Censorship of the Movies: The Social and Political Control of a Mass Medium
Madison, Wisc.: U. of Wisc. Press, 1968

Ricketson, Frank H.
Management of Motion Picture Theatres
N.Y.: McGraw-Hill, 1938

Roeburt, John
The Wicked and the Damned
N.Y.: Macfadden-Bartell Corp., 1963

Ross, Murray
Stars and Strikes: Unionization in Hollywood
N.Y.: AMS Press, 1941

Rucker, Bryce W.
The First Freedom
Carbondale, Ill.: S. Ill. U. Press, 1968

Sargent, Epes W.
Picture Theatre Advertising
N.Y.: Moving Picture World, 1915

Schillaci, Anthony
Movies and Morals
Notre Dame, Ind.: Fides Pubs., 1968

Schmidt, Georg, Werner Schmalenbach and Peter Bachlin
The Film: Its Economic, Social, and Artistic Problems
London: Falcon, 1948

Schumach, Murray
The Face on the Cutting Room Floor
N.Y.: Wm. Morrow, 1964

Seabury, William M.
Motion Picture Problems
N.Y.: Avondale Press, 1929

Shuttleworth, Frank K. and Mark A. May
The Social Conduct and Attitudes of Movie Fans
N.Y.: Arno, 1970 (rp.)

Spatz, Jonas
Hollywood in Fiction: Some Versions of the American Myth
N.Y.: Humanities Press, 1970

Spraos, John
The Decline of the Cinema: An Economist's Report
London: Allen & Unwin, 1962

Sumner, Robert L.
Hollywood Cesspool: A Startling Survey of Movieland Lives and Morals, Pictures, and Results
Wheaton, Ill.: Sword of the Lord Pubs., 1955

Terrou, Fernand and Lucien Solal
Legislation for Press, Film and Radio: Comparative Study of the Main Types of Regulations Governing the Information Media
Paris: UNESCO, 1951

Tyler, Parker
Sex Psyche Etcetera in the Film
N.Y.: Horizon, 1969

Vizzard, Jack
See No Evil: Life inside a Hollywood Censor
N.Y.: Simon & Schuster, 1970

Walker, Alexander
The Celluloid Sacrifice: Aspects of Sex in the Movies
N.Y.: Hawthorn Bks., 1967

Walker, Alexander
Sex in the Movies
Baltimore: Penguin, 1969

White, David M. and Richard Averson
Sight, Sound, and Society: Motion Pictures and Television in America
Boston: Beacon, 1968

Wolfenstein, Martha and Nathan Leites
Movies: A Psychological Study
Glencoe, Ill.: Free Press, 1950

Wollen, Peter (ed.)
Working Papers on the Cinema: Sociology and Semiology
London: British Film Inst., 1969

Young, Donald R.
Motion Pictures: A Study in Social Legislation
N.Y.: Jerome S. Ozer, 1971 (rp.)

CATEGORY 6: NATIONAL CINEMAS

Anderson, Joseph L. and Donald Richie
The Japanese Film: Art and Industry
N.Y.: Grove, 1959

Armes, Roy
French Cinema Since 1946
  Volume One: The Great Tradition
  Volume Two: The Personal Style
N.Y.: Barnes, 1966

Armes, Roy
Patterns of Realism: Neo-Realism in Italian Cinema
Cranbury, N.J.: Barnes, 1971

Arossev, A. (ed.)
Soviet Cinema
Moscow: Voks, 1935

Babitsky, Paul and John Rimberg
The Soviet Film Industry
N.Y.: Praeger, 1955

Balcon, Michael, Ernest Lindgren, Roger Manvell, and Forsyth Hardy
Twenty Years of British Film, 1925-1945
London: Falcon, 1947

Barnouw, Erik and S. Krishnaswamy
The Indian Film
N.Y.: Columbia U. Press, 1963

Baxter, John
Australian Cinema
San Francisco: Tri-Ocean, 1970

Bloem, Walter S.
The Soul of the Moving Picture
N.Y.: Dutton, 1924

Boost, C.
Dutch Art Today: Film
Amsterdam: Contact, 1958

British Film Inst.
Fifty Years of Soviet Cinema 1917-1967
London: British Film Inst., 1967

Brož, Jaroslav
The Path of Fame of the Czechoslovak Film
Prague: Czechoslovak Filmexport, 1965

Brunel, Adrian
Nice Work: The Story of Thirty Years in British Film Production
London: Forbes Robertson, 1949

Bryher, (pseud.)
Film Problems of Soviet Russia
Territot, Switzerland: Riant Chateau, 1929

Bucher, Felix
Germany: An Illustrated Guide
N.Y.: Barnes, 1969

Byrne, Richard B.
Films of Tyranny: Shot Analyses of "The Cabinet of Dr. Caligari," "The Golem" and "Nosferatu"
Madison, Wisc.: College Printing & Typing Co., 1966

Cameron, Ian (ed.)
Second Wave
N.Y.: Praeger, 1970

Carter, Huntley
The New Spirit in the Russian Theatre 1917-1928
N.Y.: Arno, 1970 (rp.)

Carter, Huntley
The New Theatre and Cinema of Soviet Russia
N.Y.: Arno, 1970 (rp.)

Casas, Vizcaino
Spanish Films
Madrid: Spanish Pubs., 1965

Contemporary Polish Cinematography
Warsaw: Polonia Pub. House, 1962

Cowie, Peter
Sweden 1: An Illustrated Guide
N.Y.: Barnes, 1969

Cowie, Peter
Sweden 2: An Illustrated Guide
N.Y.: Barnes, 1969

Cowie, Peter
Swedish Cinema
N.Y.: Barnes,

Dadoul, Georges
British Creators of Film Technique: British Scenario Writers, the Creators of the Language of D. W. Griffith, G. A. Smith, Alfred Collines, and Some Others
London: British Film Inst., 1948

Dickinson, Thorold and Catherine de la Roche
Soviet Cinema
London: Falcon, 1948

Durgnat, Raymond
Nouvelle Vague: The First Decade
Loughton, Essex: Motion Pubs., 1963

Eisner, Lotte H.
The Haunted Screen: Expressionism in the German Cinema and the Influence of Max Reinhardt
Berkeley: U. of Cal. Press, 1969

Field, Mary
Good Company: The Story of the Children's Entertainment Film Movement in Great Britain, 1943-1950
N.Y.: Longmans, Green, 1952

Film Centre, London
The Film Industry in Six European Countries: A Detailed Study of the Film Industry in Denmark as Compared with That in Norway, Sweden, Italy, France and the United Kingdom
Paris: UNESCO, 1950

Fowler, Roy
The Film in France
London: Pendulum Pubs., 1946

Freeman, Joseph, Joshu Kunitz and L. Lozowick
Voices of October: Art and Literature in Soviet Russia
N.Y.: Vanguard, 1930

Gifford, Denis
British Cinema: An Illustrated Guide
N.Y.: Barnes, 1969

Graham, Peter (comp.)
The New Wave: Critical Landmarks
Garden City, N.Y.: Doubleday, 1968

Greenhill, Leslie P. and John Tyo
Instructional Film Production, Utilization, and Research in Great Britain, Canada, and Australia
Port Washington, N.Y.: Office of Naval Research, 1949

Grodzicki, August and Irena Merz
Ten Years of People's Poland: Theatre, Film
Warsaw: Polonia Pub. House, 1955

Grzelecki, Stanisław
Polish Films Today
Warsaw: Polonia Pub. House, 1966

Guback, Thomas H.
The International Film Industry: Western Europe and America Since 1945
Bloomington, Ind.: U. of Ind. Press, 1969

Hardy, Forsyth
Scandanavian Film
London: Falcon, 1952

Hibbin, Nina
Eastern Europe: An Illustrated Guide
Cranbury, N.J.: Barnes, 1969

Holmes, Winifred (ed.)
Orient, A Survey of Films Produced in Countries of Arab and Asian Culture
London: British Film Inst., 1959

Honigmann, John J. and Marguerite van Doorslaer
Some Themes from Indian Film Reviews
Chapel Hill, N.C.: U. of N.C., 1955

Houston, Penelope
The Contemporary Cinema
Baltimore: Penguin, 1963

Hull, David S.
Film in the Third Reich: A Study of the German Cinema, 1933-1945
Berkeley: U. of Cal. Press, 1969

Idestam-Almquist, Bengt and Victor Sjöström
Classics of the Swedish Cinema
Stockholm: Swedish Inst., 1952

Jain, Rikhab D.
The Economic Aspects of the Film Industry in India
Delhi: Atma Ram, 1960

Jarratt, Vernon
The Italian Cinema
N.Y.: Macmillan, 1951

Kabir, Alamgir
The Cinema in Pakistan
Dacca: Sandhani Pubs., 1969

Khan, Mohamed
An Introduction to the Egyptian Cinema
London: Informatics, 1969

Kidd, J. Roby
Pictures with a Purpose: The Distribution of Non-Theatrical Films in Canada
Toronto: Canadian Assn. for Adult Education, 1953

Kracauer, Siegfried
Caligari to Hitler: A Psychological History of the German Film
Princeton, N.J.: Princeton U. Press, 1966 (rp.)

Landau, Jacob M.
Studies in the Arab Theater and Cinema
Philadelphia: U. of Penna. Press, 1958

Lauritzen, Einar
Swedish Films
N.Y.: Museum of Modern Art, 1962

Lebedev, Nikolai A.
Outline of the History of the Movie in the USSR
Moscow: Soshivoizdal, 1947

Leyda, Jay
Kino: A History of the Russian and Soviet Film
N.Y.: Macmillan, 1960

Low, Rachel
The History of the British Film (1896-1906, 1906-1914, 1914-1918) (3 vols.)
London: Allen & Unwin, 1948, 1949, 1950

Malerba, Luigi and Carmine Siniscalco (eds.)
Fifty Years of Italian Cinema
Rome: Carlor Bestetti, 1954

Manvell, Roger
New Cinema in Britain
N.Y.: Dutton, 1969

Manvell, Roger
New Cinema in Europe
N.Y.: Dutton, 1966

Manvell, Roger and H. Fraenkel
German Cinema
N.Y.: Praeger, 1971

Marshall, Herbert
Soviet Cinema
London: Russia Today, 1945

Martin, Marcel
France: An Illustrated Guide
N.Y.: Barnes, 1969

Mayer, Jakob P.
British Cinemas and Their Audiences
London: Dennis Dobson, 1948

Mayer, Michael F.
Foreign Films on American Screens
N.Y.: Arno, 1965 (rp.)

Modern Czechoslovak Film, 1945-1965
Prague: Czechoslovak Film Inst., 1965

Morris, Peter and Larry Kardish
Canadian Feature Films, 1914-1964
Ottawa: Canadian Film Inst., 1965

Morton-Williams, P.
Cinema in Rural Nigeria
Lagos: Federal Info. Service, 195?

Neergaard, Ebbe (ed.)
Documentary in Denmark: One Hundred Films of Fact in War, Occupation, Liberation, Peace, 1940-1948
Copenhagen: Statens Filmcentral, 1948

Neergaard, Ebbe
Motion Pictures in Denmark
Copenhagen: Statens Filmcentral, 1948

Neergaard, Ebbe
The Story of Danish Film
Copenhagen: Danish Inst.,

Nemeskürty, István
Word and Image: History of the Hungarian Cinema
Budapest: Corvina Press, 1968

Oakley, C. A.
Where We Came in: Seventy Years of the British Film Industry
London: George Allen & Unwin, 1964

Political and Economic Planning
The British Film Industry
London: Political & Economic Planning, 1952

Rangoonwalla, Firoze (comp.)
Indian Films Index: 1912-1967
Bombay: J. Udeshi, 1968

Reininger, Lotte
Shadow Theater and Shadow Films
N.Y.: Watson-Guptil Pubs., 1970

Richie, Donald
Japanese Cinema: Film Style and National Character
Garden City, N.Y.: Doubleday, 1971

Richie, Donald
The Japanese Movie
Rutland, Ver.: Japan Publications Trading Co., 1966

Richie, Donald
Japanese Movies
Tokyo: Japan Travel Bureau, 1961

Rimberg, John D.
The Motion Picture in the Soviet Union, 1918-1952: A Sociological Analysis
Ann Arbor, Mich.: Univ. Microfilms, 1959

Rondi, Gian L.
Italian Cinema Today, 1952-1965
N.Y.: Hill & Wang, 1965

Sadoul, Georges
French Film
London: Falcon, 1953

Shah, Panna
The Indian Film
Bombay: Motion Picture Society of India, 1950

Soviet Films 1938-1939
Moscow: State Pub. House for Cinema Literature, 1939

Svensson, Arne
Japan
N.Y.: Barnes, 1970

Twenty Years of Cinema in Venice
Rome: Edizioni Dell'Ateneo, 1952 (?)

Tyler, Parker
Classics of the Foreign Film
N.Y.: Citadel, 1962

Whyte, A.
New Cinema in Eastern Europe
N.Y.: Dutton, 1971

Wlaschin, Ken
Italian Cinema Since the War
N.Y.: Barnes, 1970

Wollenberg, H. H.
Fifty Years of German Film
London: Falcon, 1947

CATEGORY 7: FILM SCRIPTS

Agee, James
Agee on Film: Vol. 2, Five Film Scripts
Boston: Beacon, 1964

Anderson, Lindsay and David Sherwin
If . . .
N.Y.: Simon & Schuster, 1969

Anderson, Lindsay (ed.)
Making a Film: The Story of "Secret People"
London: Allen & Unwin, 1952

Anderson, Maxwell and Andrew Solt
Joan of Arc
N.Y.: W. Sloane, 1948

Antonioni, Michelangelo
Blow-Up
N.Y.: Simon & Schuster, 1970

Antonioni, Michelangelo
Antonioni: Four Screenplays
N.Y.: Grossman, 1971

Antonioni, Michelangelo
L'avventura: A Film, by Michelangelo Antonioni
N.Y.: Grove Press, 1969

Antonioni, Michaelangelo
Screenplays
N.Y.: Orion, 1963

Antonioni, Michaelangelo
Zabriskie Point
N.Y.: Simon & Schuster, 1971

Axel, Gabriel
Danish Blue
N.Y.: Grove,

Bass, Ulrich
Young Aphrodites
N.Y.: Stein & Day, 1966

Beckett, Samuel
Cascando
N.Y.: Grove, 1969

Beckett, Samuel
Film, A Film Script
N.Y.: Grove, 1969

Bellocchio, Marco
Bellocchio's China Is Near
N.Y.: Orion, 1969

Bergman, Ingmar
A Film Trilogy
N.Y.: Orion, 1967

Bergman, Ingmar
Four Screenplays by Ingmar Bergman
N.Y.: Simon & Schuster, 1960

Bergman, Ingmar
Seventh Seal
N.Y.: Simon & Schuster,

Bergman, Ingmar
Three Films: Through a Glass Darkly, Winter Light, The Silence
N.Y.: Grove, 1969

Bergman, Ingmar
Wild Strawberries
N.Y.: Simon & Schuster, 1969

Blacker, I. R.
Best Film Plays, 1970-1971
L.A.: Nash Pub. Co., 1971

Bolt, Robert
Doctor Zhivago: The Screen Play
N.Y.: Random House, 1966

Booker, Bob and George Foster
Pardon Me, Sir, But Is My Eye Hurting Your Elbow?
N.Y.: Random House, 1968

Buñuel, Luis
Belle de Jour
N.Y.: Simon & Schuster, 1970

Buñuel, Luis
Exterminating Angel
N.Y.: Simon & Schuster,

Buñuel, Luis
L'Age d'Or and Un Chien Andalou
N.Y.: Simon & Schuster, 1969

Buñuel, Luis
Three Screenplays
N.Y.: Orion, 1969

Buñuel, Luis
Tristana
N.Y.: Simon & Schuster, 1971

Carné, Marcel
Children of Paradise
N.Y.: Simon & Schuster, 1969

Carné, Marcel
Le Jour se Leve
London: Lorrimer,

Cassavetes, John
Faces
N.Y.: New American Lib.,

Chayefsky, Paddy
The Bachelor Party: A Screenplay
N.Y.: New American Lib., 1957

Chayefsky, Paddy
The Goddess: A Screenplay
N.Y.: Simon & Schuster, 1958

Clair, René
Four Screenplays: Le Silence d'Or, Le Beaute du Diable, Les Belles-de-Nuit, Les Grand Manouvres
N.Y.: Orion, 1970

Clair, René
A Nous la Liberte and Entr'Acte
N.Y.: Simon & Schuster, 1970

Cocteau, Jean
The Blood of a Poet
N.Y.: Bodley Press, 1949

Cocteau, Jean
Screenplays and Other Writings
   on the Cinema
N. Y.: Orion, 1968

Cocteau, Jean
Two Screenplays: The Blood of a
   Poet; The Testament of
   Orpheus
N. Y.: Orion, 1968

Culkin, John
Julius Caesar: As a Play and a
   Film
N. Y.: Scholastic Bks., 1963

Decker, Richard G. (ed.)
Plays for Our Time: Motion Pictures, Television, Radio
N. Y.: Oxford Bk. Co., 1959

de Sica, Vittorio
Bicycle Thief
N. Y.: Simon & Schuster,

de Sica, Vittorio
Miracle in Milan
Baltimore: Penguin, 1969

Dreyer, Carl T.
Four Screenplays
Bloomington, Ind.: Ind. U.
   Press, 1970

Duras, Marguerite
Hiroshima Mon Amour
N. Y.: Grove, 1961

Duras, Marguerite
Hiroshima Mon Amour and Une
   Aussi Longue Absence
Liverpool: F. L. Calder,

Eastman, Charles
All American Boy
N. Y.: Noonday, 1971

Eastman, Charles
Little Fauss and Big Halsy
N. Y.: Noonday, 1970

Eisenstein, Sergei M.
Ivan the Terrible
N. Y.: Simon & Schuster, 1962

Eisenstein, Sergei M.
Potemkin
N. Y.: Simon & Schuster, 1968

Eisenstein, Sergei M.
Que Viva Mexico!
N. Y.: Arno, 1971 (rp.)

Feibleman, James
The Margitist
New Orleans: River Press, 1945

Fellini, Federico
8 1/2
N. Y.: Ballantine, 1969

Fellini, Federico
Fellini's Early Screenplays
N. Y.: Grossman, 1970

Fellini, Federico
Fellini's Satyricon
N. Y.: Ballantine, 1970

Fellini, Federico
Juliet of the Spirits
N. Y.: Ballantine, 1966

Fellini, Federico
La Dolce Vita
N. Y.: Ballantine, 1961

Fellini, Federico
La Strada
N.Y.: Ballantine, 1970

Fellini, Federico
Three Screenplays: I Vitelloni,
 Il Bidone, The Temptations of
 Dr. Antonio
N.Y.: Orion, 1970

Fonda, Peter, Dennis Hopper
 and Terry Southern
Easy Rider
N.Y.: New American Lib., 1969

Foote, Horton
The Screenplay of To Kill a
 Mockingbird
N.Y.: Harcourt, Brace &
 World, 1964

Ford, John
Stagecoach
N.Y.: Simon & Schuster, 1970

Fry, Christopher
The Bible
N.Y.: Pocket Bks., 1966

Garret, George P., O.B.
 Hardison, Jr. and Jane
 Gelfann (eds.)
Film Scripts One
N.Y.: Appleton-Century-Crofts,
 1971

Garret, George P., O.B.
 Hardison, Jr. and Jane
 Gelfann (eds.)
Film Scripts Two
N.Y.: Appleton-Century-Crofts,
 1971

Gassner, John and Dudley
 Nichols (eds.)
Best Film Plays of 1943-44
N.Y.: Crown, 1945

Gassner, John and Dudley
 Nichols (eds.)
Best Film Plays of 1945
N.Y.: Crown, 1946

Gassner, John and Dudley
 Nichols (eds.)
Best Film Plays of 1946
N.Y.: Crown, 1947

Gassner, John and Dudley
 Nichols (eds.)
Great Film Plays
N.Y.: Crown, 1959

Gassner, John and Dudley
 Nichols (eds.)
Twenty Best Film Plays
N.Y.: Crown, 1943

Ginsberg, Milton M.
Coming Apart
N.Y.: Lancer Bks.,

Godard, Jean-Luc
Alphaville
London: Lorrimer, 1966

Godard, Jean-Luc
Le Petit Soldat
London: Lorrimer,

Godard, Jean-Luc
Made in U.S.A.
London: Lorrimer,

Godard, Jean-Luc
Masculine-Feminine
N.Y.: Grove, 1969

Godard, Jean-Luc
Pierrot le Fou
N.Y.: Simon & Schuster, 1969

Godard, Jean-Luc
Weekend
N.Y.: Simon & Schuster, 1971

Goldman, James
The Lion in Winter
N.Y.: Random House, 1966

Greene, Graham and Carol Reed
The Third Man
N.Y.: Simon & Schuster,

Hammond, R. M.
Cocteau: Beauty and the Beast
N.Y.: N.Y.U. Press, 1970

von Harbou, Thea
M; Directed by Fritz Lang: Scenario and Dialogue by Thea von Harbou
London: Lorrimer, 1968

Hellman, Lillian
North Star
N.Y.: Viking, 1943

Huston, John
Frankie and Johnny
N.Y.: Benjamin Blom, 1968

Hutchins, Robert
Zuckerkandl
N.Y.: Grove, 1969

Jacobs, Lewis
Film Writing Forms: Six Sample Scripts
N.Y.: Gotham Bk. Mart, 1934

John, Errol
Force Majeure, The Dispossessed, Hasta Luego
London: Faber, 1967

Johnston, W. et al
Klute
N.Y.: Paperback Lib., 1971

Kerouac, Jack
Pull My Daisy
N.Y.: Grove, 1961

King, David
Butch Cassidy and the Sundance Kid
N.Y.: Paperback Lib., 1970

Kronhausen, Phyllis and Eberhard Kronhausen
Freedom to Love
N.Y.: Grove, 1971

Kurosawa, Akira
Ikiru
N.Y.: Simon & Schuster,

Kurosawa, Akira
Rashomon, A Film by Akira Kurosawa
N.Y.: Grove, 1969

Kurosawa, Akira
Seven Samurai
N.Y.: Simon & Schuster, 1970

Lamorisse, Albert
White Mane
N.Y.: Dutton, 1954

Lang, Fritz
M
N.Y.: Simon & Schuster,

Lang, Fritz
Metropolis
N.Y.: Simon & Schuster, 1970

LeLouche, Claude
A Man and a Woman
N.Y.: Simon & Schuster, 1970

Lewis, Sinclair and Dore Schary
Storm in the West
N.Y.: Stein & Day, 1963

Lorentz, Pare
The River: A Scenario
N.Y.: Stackpole & Sons, 1938

Lustig, Ernst
Life Is a Song: A Script for a Musical Motion Picture or Stage Production
N.Y.: William-Frederick Press, 1951

Mankiewicz, Joseph L.
All about Eve, a Screenplay
N.Y.: Random House, 1951

Mann, Abby
Judgment at Nuremberg
London: Cassell, 1961

Maugham, William Somerset
Encore
Garden City, N.Y.: Doubleday, 1952

Maugham, William Somerset
Trio
Garden City, N.Y.: Doubleday, 1950

Mayer, D.
Eisenstein's Potemkin
N.Y.: Grossman, 1971

Maysles, Albert, David Maysles and Charlotte Zwerin
Salesman
N.Y.: New American Lib.,

McBride, Jim and I. Kit Carson
David Holzman's Diary
N.Y.: Noonday, 1970

McConville, Bernard
The Gentleman on Horseback
N.Y.: Trayor Lane, 1935

McCoy, Horace
They Shoot Horses, Don't They?
N.Y.: Avon, 1969

Menzel, Jiri
Closely Watched Trains
N.Y.: Simon & Schuster, 1970

Noble, Lorraine (ed.)
Four Star Scripts
Garden City, N.Y.: Doubleday, Doran, 1936

Osborne, John
Tom Jones
N.Y.: Grove, 1964

Pabst, G.W.
Pandora's Box
N.Y.: Simon & Schuster, 1970

Pasolini, Pier P.
Oedipus Rex
N.Y.: Simon & Schuster, 1970

Patterson, Frances T. (ed.)
Motion Picture Continuities
N.Y.: Columbia U. Press, 1929

Penn, Arthur and Venable Herndon
Alice's Restaurant
Garden City, N.Y.: Doubleday, 1970

Perry, Eleanor
The Swimmer
N.Y.: Stein & Day, 1967

Pinter, Harold
The Lover, Tea Party, The Basement
N.Y.: Grove, 1967

Prevert, J. and Marcel Carné
Jour Se Leve
N.Y.: Simon & Schuster, 1970

Pudovkin, V. I.
Mother
N.Y.: Simon & Schuster, 1970

Raphael, Frederic
Two for the Road, a Screenplay
N.Y.: Holt, Rinehart & Winston, 1967

Rattigan, Terence
The Prince and the Showgirl: The Script for the Film
N.Y.: New American Lib., 1957

Raucher, Herman
Watermelon Man
N.Y.: Ace, 1970

Reid, Alastair
To Be Alive!
N.Y.: Macmillan, 1966

Renoir, Jean
Grand Illusion
N.Y.: Simon & Schuster, 1968

Renoir, Jean
Rules of the Game
N.Y.: Simon & Schuster, 1969

Robbe-Grillet, Alain
Last Year at Marienbad
N.Y.: Grove, 1962

Schulberg, Budd
Across the Everglades: A Play for the Screen
N.Y.: Random House, 1958

Schulberg, Budd
A Face in the Crowd: A Play for the Screen
N.Y.: Random House, 1957

Semprin, Jorge
La Guerre Est Finie
N.Y.: Grove, 1968

Shaw, George Bernard
Major Barbara: A Screen Version
N.Y.: Penguin, 1946

Shaw, George Bernard
Saint Joan: A Screenplay
Seattle: U. of Wash. Press, 1968

Sheehan, Perley P.
King Arthur: A Screenplay
L.A.: Mary P. Bagg, 1936

Sjoman, Vilgot
I Am Curious (Blue)
N.Y.: Grove, 1970

Sjoman, Vilgot
I Am Curious (Yellow)
N.Y.: Grove, 1968

Sontag, Susan
Duet for Cannibals
N.Y.: Noonday, 1970

Steinbeck, John
The Forgotten Village
N.Y.: Viking, 1941

von Sternberg, Josef
The Blue Angel
N.Y.: Simon & Schuster, 1968

von Stroheim, Erich
Greed
N.Y.: Simon & Schuster, 1970

Teshigahara, Hiroshi
Woman in the Dunes
N.Y.: Phaedra, 1966

Thomas, Dylan
The Doctor and the Devils
London: Dent, 1953

Thomas, Dylon
Doctor and the Devils and Other Scripts
N.Y.: New Directions, 1970

Thompson, Lawrence C. et al
Ballad of a Soldier
N.Y.: Harcourt, Brace & World,

Trotti, Lamar and Sonya Levien
In Old Chicago
Beverly Hills, Cal.: Twentieth-Century-Fox Film Corp., 1937

Truffaut, Francois
The 400 Blows
N.Y.: Grove, 1969

Truffaut, Francois
Jules and Jim
N.Y.: Simon & Schuster, 1968

Visconti, Luchino
Visconti, Five Screenplays
   Volume 1: Terra Trema and Senso
   Volume 2: White Nights, Rocco and His Brothers, Job
N.Y.: Orion, 1969

Visconti, Luchino
Visconti; Three Screenplays: White Nights, Rocco and His Brothers, The Job
N.Y.: Orion, 1970

Visconti, Luchino
Visconti; Two Screenplays: La Terra Tremo, Senso
N.Y.: Orion, 1970

Wailland, Roger, Roger Vadim and Claude Brule
Roger Vadim's Les Liaisons Dangereuses
N.Y.: Ballantine, 1962

Warhol, Andy
"a"
N.Y.: Grove, 1970

Watkins, Peter
The War Game
London: Sphere Bks., 1967

Weine, Robert
The Cabinet of Doctor Caligari
N.Y.: Simon & Schuster, 1969

Welles, Orson
The Trial
N.Y.: Simon & Schuster, 1970

Wexler, Norman
Joe
N.Y.: Avon, 1970

Whately, Roger
The Silver Streak: A Screen Play
L.A.: Haskell-Travers, 1935

Wilder, Billy and I. A. L.
   Diamond
The Apartment and The Fortune
   Cookie
N.Y.: Praeger, 1971

Wilder, Billy and I. A. L.
   Diamond
Irma La Douce: A Screenplay
N.Y.: Tower Pubs., 1963

Wilk, Max
Yellow Submarine
N.Y.: New American Lib., 1968

Williams, Tennessee
Baby Doll: The Script for the
   Film
N.Y.: New Directions, 1956

Wurlitzer, R. and W. Corry
Two-Lane Blacktop
N.Y.: Award House Bks., 1971

CATEGORY 8: PARTICULAR FILMS

Agel, Jerome (ed.)
The Making of Kubrick's 2001
N.Y.: New American Lib., 1970

Aitken, Roy E. and Al P. Nelson
The Birth of a Nation
Middleburg, Va.: Denlinger, 1965

Anderson, Lindsay (ed.)
Making a Film: The Story of "Secret People"
London: Allen & Unwin, 1952

Barkas, Natalie
Behind the Camera
London: G. Bles, 1934
("Palaver")

Barkas, Natalie
Thirty Thousand Miles for the Films: The Story of the Filming of Soldiers Three and Rhodes of Africa
London: Blackie & Son, 1937

Beaton, Cecil
Cecil Beaton's Fair Lady
N.Y.: Holt, Reinhart & Winston, 1964

Biberman, Herbert
Salt of the Earth: The Story of a Film
Boston: Beacon, 1965

Brodsky, Jack and Nathan Weiss
The Cleopatra Papers: A Private Correspondence
N.Y.: Simon & Schuster, 1963

Brom, John L.
The Pitiless Jungle
N.Y.: D. McKay Co., 1955

Brownlow, Kevin
How It Happened Here
N.Y.: Doubleday, 1968

Buck, Frank
Wild Cargo
N.Y.: Simon & Schuster, 1932

Byrne, Richard B.
Films of Tyranny: Shot Analyses of "The Cabinet of Dr. Caligari," "The Golem" and "Nosferatu"
Madison, Wisc.: College Printing and Typing Co., 1966

Cocteau, Jean
Diary of a Film
N.Y.: Roy Pubs., 1950
("La Belle et la Bête")

Collier, John W.
A Film in the Making
London: World Film Pubs., 1947
("It Always Rains on Sunday")

Cooper, Merian C.
Grass
N.Y.: G. P. Putnam's Sons, 1925

Couffer, Jack
Song of Wild Laughter
N.Y.: Simon & Schuster, 1963

Crisler, Lois
Arctic Wild
N.Y.: Harper, 1958

Cross, Brenda (ed.)
The Film Hamlet
London: Saturn Press, 1948

Curry, George
Copperfield '70: The Story of the Making of the Omnibus-20th-Century-Fox Film
N.Y.: Ballantine, 1970

Deans, Marjorie
Meeting at the Sphinx
London: Macdonald, 1946
("Caesar and Cleopatra")

DeAntonio, Emile and Daniel Talbot
Point of Order! A Documentary of the Army-McCarthy Hearings
N.Y.: Norton, 1964

Di Franco, Philip (ed.)
Hard Day's Night, with the Beatles: A Director's Handbook
N.Y.: Chelsea House Pubs., 1970

Eliot, T. S. and George Hoellering
The Film of Murder in the Cathedral
N.Y.: Harcourt, Brace and Co., 1952

Flaherty, Frances H.
Elephant Dance
N.Y.: C. Scribner's Sons, 1937

Foreman, Carl
A Cast of Lions: The Story of the Filming of "Born Free"
London: Collins, 1966

Forman, Harrison
Horizon Hunter
N.Y.: R. M. McBride, 1940
("Lost Horizon")

Gehrts, M.
A Camera Actress in the Wilds of Togoland
London: Service & Co., 1915

Gibbon, Monk
The Tales of Hoffman, a Study of the Film
London: Saturn Press, 1951

Goode, James
The Story of The Misfits
Indianapolis: Bobbs-Merrill, 1963

Gottesman, Ronald (ed.)
Focus on Citizen Kane
Englewood Cliffs, N.J.: Prentice-Hall, 1971

Griffith, Richard
Anatomy of a Motion Picture
N.Y.: St. Martin's Press, 1959
("Anatomy of a Murder")

Hamblett, Charles
The Crazy Kill, a Fantasy
London: Sidgwich & Jackson, 1956
("Moby Dick")

Huff, Theodore
Intolerance: Shot-by-Shot Analysis
N.Y.: Museum of Modern Art, 1966

Huff, Theodore
A Shot Analysis of D. W. Griffith's The Birth of a Nation
N.Y.: Museum of Modern Art, 1961

Hughes, Eileen L.
On the Set of Fellini's Satyricon: A Behind-the-Scenes Diary
N.Y.: Wm. Morrow, 1970

Huss, R. (ed.)
Focus on Blow-Up
Englewood Cliffs, N.J.: Prentice-Hall, 1971

Hutton, Clayton
Macbeth, the Making of the Film
London: Parrish, 1960

James, David
Scott of the Antarctic: The Film and Its Production
London: Convoy Pubs., 1949

Jay, John M.
Any Old Lion
London: Frewin, 1966
("Born Free")

Johnson, Martin
Camera Trails in Africa
N.Y.: Century Co., 1924

Jones, Lon
Barabbas: The Story of a Motion Picture
Bologna: Cappelli, 1962

Malanga, Gerard and Andy Warhol
Screen Tests: A Diary
N.Y.: Kulchur Press, 1967

McClelland, C. K. and D. W. Cannon
On Making of a Movie: Brewster McCloud
N.Y.: New American Lib., 1971

McKenna, Virginia
Some of My Friends Have Tails
N.Y.: Harcourt Brace Jovanovitch, 1970
("Ring of Bright Water")

Mosley, Leonard
Battle of Britain: The Making of a Film
N.Y.: Ballantine, 1969

Mullen, Pat
Man of Aran
Cambridge, Mass.: MIT Press, 1970

Noerdlinger, Henry S.
Moses and Egypt: The Documentation to the Motion Picture The Ten Commandments
L.A.: U. of S. Cal. Press, 1956

Perry, Edward S.
A Contextual Study of Michelangelo Antonioni's Film L'Eclisse
Iowa City, Ia.: U. of Ia., 1968

Powell, Michael
200,000 Feet: The Edge of the
　　World
N.Y.: Dutton, 1938

Ross, Lillian
Picture: The Making of John
　　Huston's The Red Badge of
　　Courage
N.Y.: Avon, 1969

St. Pierre, Brian
The Fantastic Plastic Voyage
N.Y.: Coward-McCann, 1969

Schary, Dore
Case History of a Movie
N.Y.: Random House, 1950
("The Next Voice You Hear")

Silva, F. (ed.)
Focus on The Birth of a Nation
Englewood Cliffs, N.J.:
　　Prentice-Hall, 1972

Sjoman, Vilgot
I Was Curious: Diary of the
　　Making of a Film
N.Y.: Grove, 1968

Southern, Terry and William
　　Claxton
The Journal of The Loved One:
　　The Production Log of a Motion Picture
N.Y.: Random House, 1965

Stobart, Tom
I Take Pictures for Adventure
N.Y.: Doubleday, 1958

Taylor, Deems (ed.)
Walt Disney's Fantasia
N.Y.: Simon & Schuster, 1940

Van Dyke, Colonel W. S.
Horning into Africa
L.A.: Cal. Graphic Press, 1931
("Trader Horn")

Weinberg, Herman G. (ed.)
Greed
N.Y.: Arno, 1971

Wells, H. G.
The King Who Was a King, the
　　Book of a Film
London: E. Benn, 1929

Wheeler, Allen H.
Building Aeroplanes for "Those
　　Magnificent Men"
Sun Valley, Cal.: J. W. Caler,
　　1968

Whitehead, Peter and Robin Bean
　　(eds.)
Olivier, Shakespeare
London: Lorrimer, 1966
("As You Like It," "Henry V,"
　　"Hamlet," "Richard III,"
　　"Othello")

Wolfe, Maynard F.
The Making of The Adventurers
N.Y.: Paperback Lib., 1970

CATEGORY 9: PERSONALITIES, BIOGRAPHIES, AND FILMOGRAPHIES

Abbe, Patience, Richard Abbe and Johnny Abbe
Of All Places!
N.Y.: Frederick A. Stokes, 1937

Abbott, George
Mister Abbott
N.Y.: Random House, 1963

Ackerman, Forrest J.
Frankenscience Monster
N.Y.: Ace, 1969

Adams, Joey and Henry Tobias
The Borscht Belt
N.Y.: Bobbs-Merrill, 1966

Adler, Bill
I Remember Judy
Cleveland: World Pub. Co., 1970

Aherne, Brian
A Proper Job
Boston: Houghton Mifflin, 1969

Alicoate, Jack (ed.)
The Film Daily Presents Cavalcade: Yesterday, To-Day, Tomorrow of the Motion Picture Industry
N.Y.: Barnes Printing Co., 1939

Allan, John
Elizabeth Taylor: A Fascinating Story of America's Most Talented Actress and the World's Most Beautiful Woman
Derby, Conn.: Monarch Bks., 1961

Allister, Ray
Friese-Greene: Close-up of an Inventor
London: Marsland Pubs., 1948

Allvine, Glendon
The Greatest Fox of Them All
N.Y.: Lyle Stuart, 1969

Alpert, Hollis
The Barrymores
N.Y.: Dial Press, 1964

Amaral, Anthony A.
Movie Horses: Their Treatment and Training
Indianapolis: Bobbs-Merrill, 1967

Anderson, Clinton H.
Beverly Hills Is My Beat
Englewood Cliffs, N.J.: Prentice-Hall, 1960

Anderson, R. G.
Faces, Forms, Films: The Artistry of Lon Chaney
Cranbury, N.J.: Barnes, 1971

Anger, Kenneth
Hollywood Babylon
Phoenix: Associated Professional Services, 1965

Arliss, George
My Ten Years in the Studios
Boston: Little, Brown, 1940

Armes, Roy
The Cinema of Alain Resnais
N.Y.: Barnes, 1968

Armitage, Merle
Accent on America
N.Y.: E. Weyhe, 1944

Austen, David
The Cinema of Stanley Kubrick
N.Y.: Barnes, 1969

Bailey, David and Peter Evans
Good-Bye Baby and Amen
N.Y.: Coward-McCann, 1969

Baily, Francis E.
Film Stars of History
London: Macdonald, 1945

Bainbridge, John
Another Way of Living
N.Y.: Holt, Rinehart & Winston, 1969

Bainbridge, John
Garbo
Garden City, N.Y.: Doubleday, 1955

Bakeless, Katherine L.
In the Big Time
Philadelphia: Lippincott, 1953

Balcon, Michael
Michael Balcon Presents . . . A Lifetime of Films
London: Hutchinson, 1969

Ballantine, William
Wild Tigers and Tame Fleas
N.Y.: Rinehart, 1958

Ballin, Albert
The Deaf Mute Howls
L.A.: Grafton Pub. Co., 1930

Bankhead, Tallulah
Tallulah: My Autobiography
N.Y.: Harper & Bros., 1952

Barber, Walter L. and Robert Creamer
Rhubard in the Catbird Seat
Garden City, N.Y.: Doubleday, 1968

Barbour, Alan G. et al (eds.)
Karloff
Kew Gardens, N.Y.: Cinefax,

Barnett, Lincoln K.
Writing on Life: Sixteen Close-ups
N.Y.: Sloane, 1951

Barr, Charles
Laurel and Hardy
Berkeley: U. of Cal. Press, 1969

Barry, Iris
D.W. Griffith, American Film Master
Garden City, N.Y.: Doubleday, 1965 (rp.)

Barrymore, Diana and Gerold Frank
Too Much Too Soon
N.Y.: Holt, 1957

Barrymore, Elaine and Sandford Dody
All My Sins Remembered
N.Y.: Popular Lib., 1964

Barrymore, Ethel
Memories: An Autobiography
N.Y.: Kraus Reprint Co., 1968 (rp.)

Bartok, Eva
Worth Living For
N.Y.: Univ. Bks., 1959

Baxter, John
The Cinema of Josef von Sternberg
Cranbury, N.J.: Barnes, 1971

Beaton, Cecil
It Gives Me Great Pleasure
London: Weidenfeld & Nicolson, 1955

Beaton, Cecil
Photobiography
Garden City, N.Y.: Doubleday, 1951

Beaton, Cecil and Kenneth Tynan
Persona Grata
London: Wingate, 1953

Ben-Allah (pseud.)
Rudolph Valentino: His Romantic Life and Death
Hollywood: Ben-Allah Co., 1926

Bent, Silas
Ballyhoo: The Voice of the Press
N.Y.: Boni & Liveright, 1927

Bessy, M.
Orson Welles
N.Y.: Crown, 1971

Best, M.
Those Endearing Young Charms: Child Performers of the Screen
Cranbury, N.J.: Barnes, 1971

Bettina
Bettina
London: M. Joseph, 1965

Beylie, C. (ed.)
Jean Renoir Films, 1924-1939
N.Y.: Grove, 1971

Bickford, Charles
Bulls, Balls, Bicycles, and Actors
N.Y.: Paul S. Ericksson, 1965

Billquist, Fritiof
Garbo: A Biography
London: Arthur Barker, 1960

Blesh, Rudi
Keaton
N.Y.: Macmillan, 1966

Bogdanovich, Peter
Allan Dwan
N.Y.: Praeger, 1971

Bogdanovich, Peter
The Cinema of Alfred Hitchcock
N.Y.: Museum of Modern Art, 1963

Bogdanovich, Peter
The Cinema of Howard Hawks
N.Y.: Museum of Modern Art, 1962

Bogdanovich, Peter
The Cinema of Orson Welles
N.Y.: Museum of Modern Art, 1961

Bogdanovich, Peter
Fritz Lang in America
N.Y.: Praeger, 1969

Bogdanovich, Peter
John Ford
Berkeley: U. of Cal. Press, 1968

Bonomo, Joe
The Strongman: A Pictorial Autobiography
Hackensack, N.J.: Wehman Bros., 1968

Booch, Harish S. and Karing Doyle
Star-Portrait: Intimate Life Stories of Famous Film Stars
Bombay: Lakhani Bk. Depot, 1962

Booth, John B.
Pink Parade
N.Y.: Dutton, 1933

Bowman, William D.
Charlie Chaplin
N.Y.: John Day, 1931

Bowser, Eileen
The Films of Carl Dreyer
N.Y.: Museum of Modern Art, 1964

Boyarsky, William
The Rise of Ronald Reagan: A Political Biography
N.Y.: Random House, 1968

Brom, John L.
The Pitiless Jungle
N.Y.: D. McKay Co., 1955

Brown, Frederick
An Impersonation of Angels: A Biography of Jean Cocteau
N.Y.: Viking, 1968

Brown, Joe E.
Laughter Is a Wonderful Thing
N.Y.: Barnes, 1956

Brown, W.R.
Will Rogers and the American Dream
Columbia, Mo.: U. of Mo. Press, 1970

Bruno, Michael
Venus in Hollywood: The Continental Enchantress from Garbo to Loren
N.Y.: Lyle Stuart, 1970

Budgen, Suzanne
Fellini
London: British Film Inst., 1966

Bull, Clarence and Raymond Lee
The Faces of Hollywood
N.Y.: Barnes, 1969

Burbidge, Claude
Scruffy: The Adventures of a Mongrel in Movieland
London: Hurst & Blackett, 1937

Burdick, Loraine
Child Star Dolls and Toys
N.Y.: Macmillan, 1968

Burke, Billie and Cameron Shipp
With Powder on My Nose
N.Y.: Coward-McCann, 1959

Butler, Ivan
The Cinema of Roman Polanski
Cranbury, N.J.: Barnes, 1970

Cahn, William
Harold Lloyd's World of Comedy
N.Y.: Duell, Sloan & Pearce, 1964

Calder-Marshall, Arthur
The Innocent Eye: The Life of Robert J. Flaherty
N.Y.: Harcourt, Brace & World, 1963

Cameron, Ian (ed.)
The Films of Jean-Luc Godard
N.Y.: Praeger, 1970

Cameron, Ian
The Films of Robert Bresson
N.Y.: Praeger, 1970

Cameron, Ian and Elisabeth Cameron
Broads
London: Studio Vista,

Cameron, Ian and Elisabeth Cameron
Dames
N.Y.: Praeger, 1969

Cameron, Ian and Elisabeth Cameron
The Heavies
N.Y.: Praeger, 1967

Cameron, Ian and Robin Wood
Antonioni
N.Y.: Praeger, 1968

Canfield, Alyce
God in Hollywood
N.Y.: Wisdom House, 1961

Cannom, Robert C.
Van Dyke and the Mythical City, Hollywood
Culver City, Cal.: Murray & Gee, 1948

Cantor, Eddie
As I Remember Them
N.Y.: Duell, Sloan & Pearce, 1963

Cantor, Eddie
The Way I See It
Englewood Cliffs, N.J.: Prentice-Hall, 1959

Cantor, Eddie and Jane K. Ardmore
Take My Life
Garden City, N.Y.: Doubleday, 1957

Capra, Frank
Frank Capra: The Name Above the Title
N.Y.: Macmillan, 1971

Carey, Gary
The Films of George Cukor
N.Y.: Museum of Modern Art, 1970

Carmichael, Hoagy
The Stardust Road
N.Y.: Toronto, Rinehart & Co., 1946

Carmichael, Hoagy and Stephen Longstreet
Sometimes I Wonder
N.Y.: Farrar, Straus & Giroux, 1965

Carpozi, George, Jr.
The Gary Cooper Story
New Rochelle, N.Y.: Arlington House, 1970

Casty, Alan
The Films of Robert Rossen
N.Y.: Museum of Modern Art, 1969

Cerf, Bennett
Try and Stop Me
Garden City, N.Y.: Garden City Pub. Co., 1947

Chaplin, Charles
Charlie Chaplin's Own Story
Indianapolis: Bobbs-Merrill, 1916

Chaplin, Charles
My Autobiography
N.Y.: Simon & Schuster, 1964

Chaplin, Charles, Jr.
My Father Charlie Chaplin
N.Y.: Random House, 1960

Chaplin, Lita Grey
My Life with Chaplin: An Intimate Memoir
N.Y.: B. Geis, 1966

Chaplin, Michael
I Couldn't Smoke the Grass on My Father's Lawn
N.Y.: Ballantine, 1969

Chevalier, Maurice
I Remember It Well
N.Y.: Macmillan, 1970

Clair, René
Reflections on the Cinema
London: W. Kimber, 1953

Cocteau, Jean
Cocteau on Film, A Conversation Recorded by André Fraigneau
N.Y.: Roy Pubs., 1954

Cocteau, Jean
The Difficulty of Being
N.Y.: Coward-McCann, 1967

Cocteau, Jean
The Journals of Jean Cocteau
Bloomington, Ind.: Ind. U. Press, 1964

Cocteau, Jean
Professional Secrets: The Autobiography of Jean Cocteau
N.Y.: Farrar, Straus & Giroux, 1970

Cohn, Art
The Nine Lives of Michael Todd
N.Y.: Random House, 1958

Collet, Jean
Jean-Luc Godard
N.Y.: Crown, 1970

Collins, Francis A.
The Camera Man
N.Y.: Century Co., 1916

Connell, Brian
Knight Errant: A Biography of Douglas Fairbanks, Jr.
Garden City, N.Y.: Doubleday, 1955

Conway, Michael, Dion
    McGregor and Mark Ricci
The Films of Greta Garbo
N.Y.: Citadel, 1964

Conway, Michael and Mark Ricci
The Films of Jean Harlow
N.Y.: Citadel, 1965

Conway, Michael and Mark Ricci
The Films of Marilyn Monroe
N.Y.: Citadel, 1964

Cooke, Alistair
Douglas Fairbanks, the Making of
    a Screen Character
N.Y.: Museum of Modern Art,
    1940

Cooke, Alistair (ed.)
Garbo and the Night Watchmen
London: Jonathan Cape, 1937

Coplans, John, et al
Andy Warhol
Greenwich, Conn.: N.Y. Graphic
    Society, 1970

Corneau, Ernest N.
The Hall of Fame of Western
    Film Stars
North Quincy, Mass.: Christopher Pub. House, 1969

Costello, Donald P.
The Serpent's Eye: Shaw and the
    Cinema
Notre Dame, Ind.: U. of Notre
    Dame Press, 1965

Cotes, Peter and Thelma Niklaus
The Little Fellow: The Life and
    Work of Charles Chaplin
N.Y.: Citadel, 1966

Cowie, Peter
Antonioni, Bergman, Resnais
N.Y.: Barnes, 1963

Cowie, Peter
The Films of Orson Welles
N.Y.: Barnes, 1964

Crawford, Joan and Jane K.
    Ardmore
A Portrait of Joan
Garden City, N.Y.: Doubleday,
    1962

Crichton, Kyle
The Marx Brothers
Garden City, N.Y.: Doubleday,
    1950

Crisp, C.G. and M. Walker
Francois Truffaut
N.Y.: Praeger, 1971

Croce, A.
Fred Astaire Ginger Rogers
    Movie Book
N.Y.: Outerbridge & Dienstfrey,
    1971

Crosby, Bing
Call Me Lucky
N.Y.: Tavistock Pubs., 1968

Crosby, Kathryn
Bing and Other Things
N.Y.: Meredith Press, 1967

Crowther, Bosley
Hollywood Rajah: The Life and
    Times of Louis B. Mayer
N.Y.: Holt, Rinehart & Winston,
    1960

Croy, Homer
Star Maker, The Story of D. W. Griffith
N.Y.: Duell, Sloan & Pearce, 1959

Curti, Carlo
Skouras: King of Fox Studios
L.A.: Holloway House, 1967

Cussler, Margaret
Not by a Long Shot: Adventures of a Documentary Film Producer
N.Y.: Exposition Press, 1951

Dadoul, Georges
British Creators of Film Technique: British Scenario Writers, the Creators of the Language of D. W. Griffith, G. A. Smith, Alfred Collins, and Some Others
London: British Film Inst., 1948

Dandridge, Dorothy and Earl Conrad
Everything and Nothing: The Dorothy Dandridge Tragedy
N.Y.: Abelard-Schuman, 1970

Davidson, William
The Real and the Unreal
N.Y.: Harper & Row, 1961

Davis, Bette
The Lonely Life: An Autobiography
N.Y.: G. P. Putnam's Sons, 1962

Davis, Elise Miller
The Answer Is God: The Inspiring Personal Story of Dale Evans and Roy Rodgers
N.Y.: McGraw-Hill, 1955

Davis, Sammy, Jr. and Jane Boyar
Yes I Can
N.Y.: Pocket Bks., 1966

Day, Donald
Will Rogers, the Boy Roper
Boston: Houghton Mifflin, 1950

DeHavilland, Olivia
Every Frenchman Has One
N.Y.: Random House, 1962

DeMille, Agnes
Dance to the Piper
Boston: Little, Brown, 1952

DeMille, Cecil B.
The Autobiography of Cecil B. DeMille
Englewood Cliffs, N.J.: Prentice-Hall, 1959

DeMille, William C.
Hollywood Saga
N.Y.: Dutton, 1939

Deschner, Donald
The Films of Cary Grant
N.Y.: Citadel, 1971

Deschner, Donald
The Films of Spencer Tracy
N.Y.: Citadel, 1968

Deschner, Donald
The Films of W. C. Fields
N.Y.: Citadel, 1966

Dickens, Homer
The Films of Gary Cooper
N.Y.: Citadel, 1970

Dickens, Homer
The Films of Katherine Hepburn
N.Y.: Citadel, 1971

Dickens, Homer
The Films of Marlene Dietrich
N.Y.: Citadel, 1968

Donner, Jörn
The Personal Vision of Ingmar Bergman
Bloomington, Ind.: U. of Ind. Press, 1966

Douglas-Home, Robin
Sinatra
N.Y.: Grosset & Dunlap, 1962

Dressler, Marie
The Life Story of an Ugly Duckling
N.Y.: R. M. McBride, 1924

Dressler, Marie and Mildred Harrington
My Own Story
Boston: Little, Brown, 1934

Drinkwater, John
The Life and Adventures of Carl Laemmle
N.Y.: G. P. Putnam's Sons, 1931

Duncan, Peter
In Hollywood Tonight
London: Laurie, 1952

Durgnat, Raymond
Franju
Berkeley: U. of Cal. Press, 1968

Durgnat, Raymond
Luis Buñuel
Berkeley: U. of Cal. Press, 1968

Durgnat, Raymond and John Kobal
Greta Garbo
N.Y.: Dutton, 1965

Dwiggins, Don
Hollywood Pilot: The Biography of Paul Montz
Garden City, N.Y.: Doubleday, 1967

Eisenstein, Sergei M.
Notes of a Film Director
London: Lawrence & Wishart, 1959

Essoe, Gabe
The Films of Clark Gable
N.Y.: Citadel, 1970

Essoe, Gabe
Tarzan of the Movies
N.Y.: Citadel, 1968

Essoe, Gabe and Ray Lee
Gable: A Complete Gallery of His Screen Portraits
L.A.: Price, Stern & Sloan, 1967

Essoe, Gabe and Raymond Lee
DeMille: The Man and His Pictures
N.Y.: Barnes, 1970

Evans, Peter
Peter Sellers: The Mask behind the Mask
Englewood Cliffs, N.J.: Prentice-Hall, 1968

Everson, William K.
The Art of W. C. Fields
Indianapolis: Bobbs-Merrill, 1967

Everson, William K.
The Bad Guys: A Pictorial History of the Movie Villain
N.Y.: Citadel, 1964

Everson, William K.
The Films of Hal Roach
N.Y.: Museum of Modern Art, 1970

Everson, William K.
The Films of Laurel and Hardy
N.Y.: Citadel, 1967

Ewers, Carolyn H.
Long Journey: A Biography of Sidney Poitier
N.Y.: New American Lib., 1969

Eyles, Allen
The Marx Brothers: Their World of Comedy
N.Y.: Barnes, 1969 (rev. ed.)

Fairbanks, Douglas
Laugh and Live
N.Y.: Briton Pub. Co., 1917

Fairweather, Virginia
Sir Laurence Olivier: An Informal Portrait
N.Y.: Coward-McCann, 1969

Fallaci, Oriana
The Egotists
N.Y.: Tempo Bks., 1963

Farrell, Barry
Pat and Roald
N.Y.: Random House, 1969

Feild, Robert D.
The Art of Walt Disney
N.Y.: Macmillan, 1942

Fenton, Robert W.
The Big Swingers
Englewood Cliffs, N.J.: Prentice-Hall, 1967

Fernett, Gene
Starring John Wayne
Cocoa, Fla.: Cinememories Pubs., 1969

Fields, W. C.
Drat!
N.Y.: New American Lib., 1969

Finler, Joel W.
Stroheim
Berkeley: U. of Cal. Press, 1968

Flaherty, Frances Hubbard
The Odyssey of a Film-Maker
Urbana, Ill.: Beta Phi Mu Chapbook, 1966

Ford, Glenn and Margaret Redfield
Glenn Ford, R.F.D. Beverly Hills
Old Tappan, N.J.: Hewitt House, 1970

Fowler, Gene
Good Night, Sweet Prince: The Life and Times of John Barrymore
N.Y.: Viking, 1944

Fowlie, Wallace
Jean Cocteau
Bloomington, Ind.: Ind. U. Press, 1966

Fox, Charles D.
Famous Film Folk
N.Y.: George H. Doran, 1925

Fox, Charles D.
Mirrors of Hollywood
N.Y.: Charles Renard Corp., 1925

Fox, Charles D. and Milton L. Silver (eds.)
Who's Who on the Screen
N.Y.: Ross Pub. Co., 1920

Frazier, George
The One with the Mustache is Costello
N.Y.: Random House, 1947

Frewin, Leslie
Blond Venus: A Life of Marlene Dietrich
London: MacGibbon & Kee, 1955

Frewin, Leslie
Dietrich
N.Y.: Stein & Day, 1967

Gable, Kathleen
Clark Gable: A Personal Portrait
Englewood Cliffs, N.J.: Prentice-Hall, 1961

Gabor, Zsa Zsa and Frank Gerold
Zsa Zsa Gabor: My Story
Cleveland: World Pub. Co., 1960

Gaither, Gant
Princess of Monaco: The Story of Grace Kelly
N.Y.: Holt, 1957

Garceau, Jean and Inez Cocke
Dear Mr. G
Boston: Little, Brown, 1961

Gargan, William
Why Me? An Autobiography
Garden City, N.Y.: Doubleday, 1969

Geduld, Harry M. (ed.)
Film Makers on Film Making
Bloomington, Ind.: Ind. U. Press, 1968

Geduld, Harry M. (ed.)
Focus on D. W. Griffith
Englewood Cliffs, N.J.: Prentice-Hall, 1971

Geduld, Harry M. and Ronald Gottesman (eds.)
Sergei Eisenstein and Upton Sinclair
Bloomington, Ind.: Ind. U. Press, 1970

Gehman, Richard
Sinatra and His Rat Pack
N.Y.: Belmont Bks., 1961

Gehman, Richard
The Tall American: The Story of Gary Cooper
N.Y.: Hawthorn Bks., 1963

Gelmis, Joseph
The Film Director as Superstar
Garden City, N.Y.: Doubleday, 1970

Gerber, Albert B.
Bashful Billionaire: The Story of
    Howard Hughes
N.Y.: Lyle Stuart, 1967

Gibson, A.
Silence of God: A Creative Response to the Films of Ingmar Bergman
N.Y.: Harper & Row, 1969

Gidal, P.
Andy Warhol
N.Y.: Dutton, 1971

Gill, Jerry H.
Ingmar Bergman and the Search for Meaning
Grand Rapids, Mich.: Wm. B. Eerdman's Pub. Co., 1969

Gilson, René
Jean Cocteau: An Investigation into His Films and Philosophy
N.Y.: Crown, 1964

Gish, Lillian and Ann Pinchot
Lillian Gish: The Movies, Mr. Griffith, and Me
Englewood Cliffs, N.J.: Prentice-Hall, 1969

Glyn, Anthony
Elinor Glyn: A Biography
London: Hutchinson, 1968

Godard, Jean-Luc
Jean-Luc Godard
N.Y.: Crown,

Godowsky, Dagmar
First Person Plural, The Lives of Dagmar Godowsky
N.Y.: Viking, 1958

Goldsmith, Warren (ed.)
Film Fame
Beverly Hills: Fame Pub. Co., 1966

Gomes, P. E.
Jean Vigo
Berkeley: U. of Cal. Press, 1971

Goodman, Ezra
Bogey--The Good Bad Guy
N.Y.: Lyle Stuart, 1965

Gorham, Maurice
Showmen and Suckers
London: Marshall, 1951

Graham, Sheilah
College of One
N.Y.: Viking, 1967

Graham, Sheilah
Confessions of a Hollywood Columnist
N.Y.: Morrow, Wm. & Co., 1969

Graham, Sheilah
The Garden of Allah
N.Y.: Crown, 1970

Graham, Sheilah
The Rest of the Story
N.Y.: Coward-McCann, 1964

Graham, Sheilah and Gerold Frank
Beloved Infidel
N.Y.: Bantam Bks., 1970

Granlund, Nils T., Sid Feder, and Ralph Hancock
Blondes, Brunettes and Bullets
N.Y.: D. McKay Co., 1957

Grierson, John
Grierson on Documentary
Berkeley: U. of Cal. Press, 1966

Griffith, Corinne
Eggs I Have Known
N.Y.: Farrar, Strauss & Cudahy, 1955

Griffith, Corinne
Hollywood Stories
N.Y.: F. Fell, 1962

Griffith, Corinne
Papa's Delicate Condition
Boston: Houghton Mifflin, 1952

Griffith, D. W.
The Rise and Fall of Free Speech in America
Hollywood: Larry Edmunds Bookshop, 1968

Griffith, Richard
The Cinema of Gene Kelly
N.Y.: Museum of Modern Art, 1962

Griffith, Richard
Marlene Dietrich: Image and Legend
N.Y.: Museum of Modern Art, 1959

Griffith, Richard
Movie Stars
Garden City, N.Y.: Doubleday, 1970

Griffith, Richard
Samuel Goldwyn: The Producer and His Films
N.Y.: Simon & Schuster, 1956

Griffith, Richard
The World of Robert Flaherty
N.Y.: Duell, Sloan & Pearce, 1953

Grossmith, George
G. G.
London: Hutchinson, 1933

Gruen, John
Close-Up
N.Y.: Viking, 1968

Guarner, Jose L.
Rossellini
N.Y.: Praeger, 1970

Guild, Leo
Hollywood's Last Tycoon
L.A.: Holloway House, 1970

Guiles, Fred L.
Norma Jean: The Life of Marilyn Monroe
N.Y.: McGraw-Hill, 1969

Halliday, Ruth S.
Stars on the Crosswalks: An Intimate Guide to Hollywood
Sherman Oaks, Cal.: Mitock & Sons, 1958

Hallowell, John
The Truth Game
N.Y.: Bantam Bks., 1969

Hamblett, Charles
Hollywood Cage
N.Y.: Hart Pub. Co., 1969

Hamblett, Charles
Who Killed Marilyn Monroe? Or, Cage to Catch Our Dreams
London: L. Frewin, 1966

Hammontree, Marie
Walt Disney: Young Movie Maker
Indianapolis: Bobbs-Merrill,

Hancock, Ralph and Letitia Fairbanks
Douglas Fairbanks--The Fourth Musketeer
N.Y.: Holt, 1953

Hanna, David
Ava, A Portrait of a Star
N.Y.: G.P. Putnam's Sons, 1960

Harding, James
Sacha Guitry: The Last Boulevardier
N.Y.: Scribners, 1968

Harman, B.
Hollywood Panorama
N.Y.: Dutton, 1971

Hart, William S.
My Life East and West
N.Y.: Benjamin Blom, 1968 (rp.)

Havoc, June
Early Havoc
N.Y.: Simon & Schuster, 1959

Hayden, Sterling
Wanderer
N.Y.: Alfred A. Knopf, 1963

Hayes, Helen and Sanford Dody
On Reflection
N.Y.: Crest Bks., 1969

Hays, Will H.
The Memoirs
Garden City, N.Y.: Doubleday, 1955

Head, Edith and Jane K. Ardmore
The Dress Doctor
Boston: Little, Brown, 1959

Hecht, Ben
Child of the Century
N.Y.: Ballantine, 1970

Henderson, Robert
D.W. Griffith: The Years at Biograph
N.Y.: Farrar, Straus & Giroux, 1970

Hepworth, Cecil M.
Came the Dawn: Memories of a Film Pioneer
London: Phoenix House, 1951

Higham, Charles
The Films of Orson Welles
Berkeley: U. of Cal. Press, 1971

Higham, Charles
Hollywood Cameramen
Bloomington, Ind.: Ind. U. Press, 1970

Higham, Charles and Joel Greenberg
The Celluloid Muse: Hollywood Directors
London: Angus & Robertson, 1969

Hodges, Bart
Life's Little Dramas
N.Y.: Duell, Sloan & Pearce, 1948

Holstius, E. Nils
Hollywood through the Back Door
N.Y.: Longmans, Green, 1937

Homoki-Nagy, István
Pals
Budapest: Corvina Press, 1961

Hope, Bob
Have Tux, Will Travel: Bob Hope's Own Story as Told to Pete Martin
N.Y.: Simon & Schuster, 1954

Hopkinson, Peter
Split Focus: An Involvement in Two Decades
London: Hart-Davis, 1969

Hopper, Hedda
From under My Hat
Garden City, N.Y.: Doubleday, 1952

Hopper, Hedda and James Brough
The Whole Truth and Nothing But
N.Y.: Pyramid Bks., 1963

Houghton, Norris
But Not Forgotten
N.Y.: Sloane, 1951

Hudson, Richard and Raymond Lee
Gloria Swanson
Cranbury, N.J.: Barnes, 1970

Huff, Theodore
Charlie Chaplin
N.Y.: Henry Schuman, 1951

Hughes, Elinor
Famous Stars of Filmdom
Boston: L. C. Page, 1932

Hughes, Elinor
Famous Stars of Filmdom (Men)
Freeport, N.Y.: Bks. for Libs. Press, 1970 (rp.)

Hughes, Elinor
Famous Stars of Filmdom (Women)
Freeport, N.Y.: Bks. for Libs. Press, 1970 (rp.)

Hughes, Laurence A. (ed.)
The Truth about the Movies by the Stars
Hollywood: Hollywood Pubs., 1924

Huntley, John
Railways in the Cinema
London: Ian Allen, 1969

Hyams, Joe
Bogie: The Biography of Humphrey Bogart
N.Y.: New American Lib.,

Irwin, William H.
The House that Shadows Built
N.Y.: Arno, 1970 (rp.)

Ivens, Joris
Camera and I
N.Y.: International Publishers, 1969

Jensen, Paul M.
The Cinema of Fritz Lang
N.Y.: Barnes, 1969

Jessel, George
Halo over Hollywood
Van Nuys, Cal.: Toastmaster Pub. Co., 1963

Jessel, George
So Help Me
N.Y.: Random House, 1943

Jessel, George
This Way, Miss
N.Y.: Holt, 1955

Johnston, Alva
The Great Goldwyn
N.Y.: Random House, 1937

Jones, Ken D., Arthur F. McClure and Alfred E. Twomey
The Films of James Stewart
N.Y.: Barnes, 1970

Kanin, G.
Tracy and Hepburn
N.Y.: Viking, 1971

Kantor, Bernard, Irwin R. Blacker and Ann Kramer
Directors at Work: Interviews with American Film Makers
N.Y.: Funk & Wagnalls, 1970

Katkov, Norman
The Fabulous Fanny: The Story of Fanny Brice
N.Y.: Knopf, 1953

Katz, Marjorie
Grace Kelly
N.Y.: Coward-McCann, 1970

Keaton, Buster and Charles Samuels
My Wonderful World of Slapstick
Garden City, N.Y.: Doubleday, 1960

Kleiner, Dick (ed.)
ESP and the Stars
N.Y.: Grosset & Dunlap, 1970

Knight, Arthur & Eliot Elisofon
The Hollywood Style
N.Y.: Macmillan, 1969

Kobal, John
Marlene Dietrich
N.Y.: Dutton,

Koury, Phil A.
Yes, Mr. DeMille
N.Y.: G.P. Putnam's Sons, 1959

Kyrou, Ado
Luis Buñuel: An Introduction
N.Y.: Simon & Schuster, 1963

Lahue, Kalton C.
Mack Sennett's Keystone: The Man, the Myth and the Comedies
Cranbury, N.J.: Barnes, 1971

Lahue, Kalton C. and Samuel Gill
Clown Princes and Court Jesters
Cranbury, N.J.: Barnes, 1970

Laing, E. E.
Greta Garbo: The Story of a Specialist
London: J. Gifford, 1946

Lake, Veronica and Donald Bain
Veronica: The Autobiography of Veronica Lake
N.Y.: Citadel, 1971

LaMarr, Hedy
Ecstasy and Me
Greenwich, Conn.: Fawcett Pubs., 1966

Lamparski, Richard
Whatever Became of . . . ?
N.Y.: Crown, 1966

Lamparski, Richard
*Whatever Became of . . . ?
(Second Series)*
N.Y.: Crown, 1968

Lamparski, Richard
*Whatever Became of . . . ?
(Third Series)*
N.Y.: Crown, 1970

Lasky, Jesse and Don Weldon
I Blow My Own Horn
Garden City, N.Y.: Doubleday, 1957

Laver, James
Between the Wars
Boston: Houghton Mifflin, 1961

Leahy, James
The Cinema of Joseph Losey
N.Y.: Barnes, 1967

Lebel, J. P.
Buster Keaton
N.Y.: Barnes,

Lee, Raymond
The Films of Mary Pickford
Cranbury, N.J.: Barnes, 1970

Lee, Raymond
Fit for the Chase: Cars and the Movies
Cranbury, N.J.: Barnes, 1969

Lee, Raymond
M
Encino, Cal.: Defilee Pubs., 1958

Lee, Raymond
Not So Dumb: Animals in the Movies
N.Y.: Barnes, 1970

Lee, Raymond and Richard M. Hudson
Gloria Swanson
N.Y.: Barnes, 1970

Lejeune, Caroline A.
Thank You for Having Me
London: Hutchinson, 1964

Leonard, Eddie
What a Life, I'm Telling You
N.Y.: E. Leonard, 1934

Leprohon, Pierre
Michelangelo Antonioni: An Introduction
N.Y.: Simon & Schuster, 1963

Le Roy, Mervyn
It Takes More than Talent
N.Y.: Alfred A. Knopf, 1953

Livingston, Don
Film and the Director: A Handbook and Guide to Film Direction
N.Y.: G. P. Putnam's Sons, 1969

Loos, Anita
A Girl Like I
N.Y.: Viking, 1966

Loos, Anita
No Mother to Guide Her
N.Y.: McGraw-Hill, 1961

Losey, Joseph and Tom Milne
Losey on Losey
Garden City, N.Y.: Doubleday,

Madsen, Axel
Billy Wilder
Bloomington, Ind.: Ind. U.
 Press, 1969

Malins, Lieut., Geoffrey H.
How I Filmed the War
London: H. Jenkins, 1920

Mallen, Frank
Sauce for the Gander
White Plains, N.Y.: Baldwin
 Bks., 1954

Maltin, Leonard
Movie Comedy Teams
N.Y.: New American Lib.,
 1970

Man, Ray
Self Portrait
Boston: Little, Brown, 1963

Manfull, Helen (ed.)
Additional Dialogue: Letters of
 Dalton Trumbo 1942-1962
Philadelphia: M. Evans, 1970

Mansfield, Jayne and Mickey
 Hargitay
Jayne Mansfield's Wild, Wild
 World
L.A.: Holloway House, 1963

Marill, A.H. et al (eds.)
Bing Crosby
Kew Gardens, N.Y.: Cinefax,

Markopoulos, Gregory J.
Quest for Serenity: Journal of a
 Film-Maker
N.Y.: Film-Makers' Cinema-
 theque, 1965

Marks, Edward B. and Abbott J.
 Liebling
They All Sang
N.Y.: Viking, 1934

Martin, M. et al (eds.)
The Complete Works of S.M.
 Eisenstein
N.Y.: Grove Press, 1971

Martin, Pete
Hollywood without Makeup
Philadelphia: Lippincott, 1948

Martin, Pete
Will Acting Spoil Marilyn
 Monroe?
Garden City, N.Y.: Doubleday,
 1956

Marx, Arthur
Life with Groucho
N.Y.: Simon & Schuster, 1954

Marx, Arthur
Not as a Crocodile
N.Y.: Harper, 1958

Marx, Groucho
Groucho and Me
N.Y.: B. Geis Associates, 1959

Marx, Groucho
The Groucho Letters
N.Y.: New American Lib., 1968

Marx, Harpo and Rowland Barber
Harpo Speaks
London: V. Gollancz, 1961

Mason, Paul
W. C. Fields: I Never Met a Kid I Liked
N. Y.: Random House, 1970

McCabe, John
Mr. Laurel and Mr. Hardy
Garden City, N. Y.: Doubleday, 1961

McCaffrey, D. W. (ed.)
Focus on Chaplin
Englewood Cliffs, N. J.: Prentice-Hall, 1971

McCaffrey, Donald
Four Great Comedians: Chaplin, Lloyd, Keaton, Langdon
N. Y.: Barnes, 1968

McCallum, John
That Kelly Family
Cranbury, N. J.: Barnes, 1957

McCarty, Clifford
Bogey: The Films of Humphrey Bogart
N. Y.: Citadel, 1965

McClure, Arthur F., Ken D. Jones and Alfred E. Twomey
The Films of James Stewart
Cranbury, N. J.: Barnes, 1970

McCrindle, Joseph F. (ed.)
Behind the Scenes: Theater and Film Interviews from the Transatlantic Review
N. Y.: Holt, Rinehart & Winston, 1970

McDonald, Gerald, Michael Conway and Mark Ricci
The Films of Charlie Chaplin
N. Y.: Citadel, 1965

McDowall, Roddy
Double Exposure
N. Y.: Delacorte Press, 1966

Meier, Nellie S.
Lion's Paws, the Story of Famous Hands
N. Y.: B. Mussey, 1937

Menjou, Adolph and M. M. Musselman
It Took Nine Tailors
N. Y.: Whittlesey House, 1948

Meyers, Warren B.
Who Is That? The Late, Late Viewers Guide to the Old, Old Movie Players
N. Y.: Personality Posters Associates, 1967

Michael, Paul
Humphrey Bogart: The Man and His Films
Indianapolis: Bobbs-Merrill, 1965

Miller, Diane Disney
The Story of Walt Disney
N. Y.: Holt, Rinehart & Winston, 1957

Miller, Edwin
Seventeen Interviews: Film Stars and Super-Stars of the Sixties
N. Y.: Macmillan, 1970

Miller, Virgil E.
Splinters from Hollywood Tripods: Memoirs of a Cameraman
N. Y.: Exposition Press, 1964

Milne, Tom
The Cinema of Carl Dreyer
Cranbury, N.J.: Barnes, 1970

Milne, Tom
Roubin Mamoulian
Bloomington, Ind.: Ind. U.
  Press, 1969

Minney, Rubeigh J.
Chaplin, the Immortal Tramp:
  The Life and Work of Charles
  Chaplin
London: Newnes, 1954

Minney, Rubeigh J.
Hollywood by Starlight
London: Chapman & Hall, 1935

Minott, Rodney G.
The Sinking of the Lollypop:
  Shirley Temple vs. Pete
  McCloskey
San Francisco: Diablo Press,
  1968

Mix, Olive Stokes and Eric
  Heath
The Fabulous Tom Mix
Englewood Cliffs, N.J.:
  Prentice-Hall, 1957

Moger, Art
Some of My Best Friends Are
  People
Boston: Challenge Press, 1964

Montagu, Ivor
With Eisenstein in Hollywood
N.Y.: International Publishing
  Co., 1969

Monti, C. and C. Rice
W. C. Fields and Me
Englewood Cliffs, N.J.:
  Prentice-Hall, 1971

Moore, Colleen
Silent Star
Garden City, N.Y.: Doubleday,
  1968

Morella, Joe and Edward Z.
  Epstein
Judy: The Films and Career of
  Judy Garland
N.Y.: Citadel, 1969

Morella, Joe and Edward Z.
  Epstein
Lana Turner
N.Y.: Citadel, 1971

Morella, Joe and Edward Z.
  Epstein
Rebels: The Rebel Hero in Films
N.Y.: Citadel, 1971

Morin, Edgar
The Stars
N.Y.: Grove, 1960

Morley, Robert and Sewell
  Stokes
Robert Morley: A Reluctant
  Biography
N.Y.: Simon & Schuster, 1966

Moussinac, Leon
Sergei Eisenstein
N.Y.: Crown, 1970

Munsterberg, Margaret
Hugo Munsterberg: His Life and
  Work
N.Y.: D. Appleton, 1922

Murphy, Senator George and Victor Lasky
Say . . . Didn't You Used to Be George Murphy?
N. Y.: Bartholomew House, 1970

Mussman, Toby (ed.)
Jean-Luc Godard: A Critical Anthology
N. Y.: Dutton, 1968

Naumburg, Nancy (ed.)
We Make the Movies
N. Y.: W. W. Norton, 1937

Negri, Pola
Memoirs of a Star
Garden City, N. Y.: Doubleday, 1970

Nemcek, Paul
The Films of Nancy Carroll
N. Y.: Lyle Stuart, 1969

Nemcek, Paul
Nancy Carroll: A Charmer's Almanac
N. Y.: Lyle Stuart, 1970

Newman, Robert
Princess Grace Kelly
Derby, Conn.: Monarch Bks., 1962

Newquist, Roy
Showcase
N. Y.: Wm. Morrow, 1966

Newquist, Roy
A Special Kind of Magic
Chicago: Rand McNally, 1967

Nichols, Beverly
The Star Spangled Manner
Garden City, N. Y.: Doubleday, Doran, 1928

Nicholson, Dianne
Turn on to Stardom
N. Y.: Cornerstone Lib.,

Niver, Kemp R.
Mary Pickford, Comedienne
L. A.: Historical Films,

Nizhny, Vladimir
Lessons with Eisenstein
N. Y.: Hill & Wang, 1962

Noble, Peter
The Fabulous Orson Welles
London: Hutchinson, 1956

Noble, Peter
Hollywood Scapegoat: The Biography of Erich von Stroheim
London: Fortune Press, 1950

Noble, Peter
Index to the Work of Alfred Hitchcock
London: British Film Inst., 1949

Noble, Peter
Profiles and Personalities
London: Brownlee, 1946

Nolan, William
John Huston, King Rebel
L. A.: Sherbourne Press, 1965

Nowell-Smith, Geoffrey
Luchino Visconti
Garden City, N. Y.: Doubleday, 1968

Oberfirst, Robert
Rudolph Valentino: The Man behind the Myth
N.Y.: Citadel, 1962

O'Brien, Pat
The Wind at My Back
Garden City, N.Y.: Doubleday, 1964

O'Brien, Patrick J.
Will Rogers, Ambassador of Good Will, Prince of Wit and Wisdom
Philadelphia: John C. Winston, 1935

O'Dell, Paul
Griffith and the Rise of Hollywood
Cranbury, N.J.: Barnes, 1970

Ohlin, Peter H.
Agee
N.Y.: I. Obolensky, 1966

Onyx, Narda
Water, World and Weismuller
L.A.: VION Pub. Co., 1964

Palmborg, Rilla P.
The Private Life of Greta Garbo
Garden City, N.Y.: Doubleday, Doran, 1931

Parish, J.R.
The Fox Girls
New Rochelle, N.Y.: Arlington House, 1971

Parish, J.R. et al (eds.)
Errol Flynn
Kew Gardens, N.Y.: Cinefax,

Parsons, Louella
The Gay Illiterate
Garden City, N.Y.: Doubleday, Doran, 1944

Parsons, Louella
Tell It to Louella
N.Y.: G.P. Putnam's Sons, 1961

Partridge, Helen
A Lady Goes to Hollywood
N.Y.: Macmillan, 1941

Pasternak, Joe and David Chandler
Easy the Hard Way
N.Y.: Putnam, 1956

Payne, Robert
The Great God Pan: A Biography of the Tramp Played by Charles Chaplin
N.Y.: Hermitage House, 1952

Pearson, George
Flashback: The Autobiography of a British Film-Maker
London: George Allen & Unwin, 1957

Peden, Charles
Newsreel Man
Garden City, N.Y.: Doubleday, Doran, 1932

Pennebaker, D.A.
Bob Dylan: Don't Look back
N.Y.: Ballantine, 1968

Perry, George
The Films of Alfred Hitchcock
N.Y.: Dutton, 1965

Petrie, Graham
The Cinema of Francois Truffaut
Cranbury, N.J.: Barnes, 1970

Pickford, Mary
My Rendezvous with Life
N.Y.: H. C. Kinsey, 1935

Pickford, Mary
Sunshine and Shadow
Garden City, N.Y.: Doubleday, 1955

Platt, Frank C. (comp.)
Great Stars of Hollywood's Golden Age
N.Y.: New American Lib., 1966

Playboy Editors (eds.)
Playboy Interviews Peter Fonda and Elliot Gould
Chicago: Playboy Press, 1971

Porter, Hal
Stars of Australian Stage and Screen
San Francisco: Tri-Ocean, 1965

Pratley, Gerald
The Cinema of John Frankenheimer
N.Y.: Barnes, 1969

Pratley, Gerald
The Cinema of Otto Preminger
Cranbury, N.J.: Barnes, 1971

Price, Vincent
I Like What I Know: A Visual Biography
Garden City, N.Y.: Doubleday, 1959

Quigley, Isabel
Charlie Chaplin: The Early Comedies
London: Studio Vista, 1968

Quirk, Lawrence J.
The Films of Fredric March
N.Y.: Citadel, 1971

Quirk, Lawrence J.
The Films of Ingrid Bergman
N.Y.: Citadel, 1970

Quirk, Lawrence J.
The Films of Joan Crawford
N.Y.: Citadel, 1968

Quirk, Lawrence J.
The Films of Paul Newman
N.Y.: Citadel, 1971

Ray, Charles
Hollywood Shorts
L.A.: Cal. Graphic Press, 1935

Reagan, Ronald and Richard G. Hubler
Where's the Rest of Me?
N.Y.: Duell, Sloan and Pearce, 1965

Rebel, Enrique J.
Great Cameramen: An Annotated Dictionary
N.Y.: Barnes, 1969

Regan, Michael
The Mansions of Beverly Hills
L.A.: Regan Pub. Co., 1966

Reynolds, Debbie and Bob Thomas
If I Knew Then
N.Y.: B. Geis Associates, 1962

Ricci, Mark, Boris Zmijewsky, and Steve Zmijewsky
The Films of John Wayne
N.Y.: Citadel, 1970

Rice, Cy
Cleopatra in Mink
N.Y.: Paperback Lib., 1962

Richards, Dick
The Life Story of Danny Kaye
London: Convoy Pubs., 1949

Richardson, Anthony
Crash Kavanagh
London: M. Parrish, 1953

Richie, Donald
The Films of Akira Kurosawa
Berkeley: U. of Cal. Press, 1966

Richie, Donald
George Stevens: An American Romantic
N.Y.: Museum of Modern Art, 1970

Ringgold, Gene
The Films of Bette Davis
N.Y.: Citadel, 1966

Ringgold, Gene and DeWitt Bodeen
The Films of Cecil B. DeMille
N.Y.: Citadel, 1969

Ringgold, Gene and Clifford McCarty
The Films of Frank Sinatra
N.Y.: Citadel, 1971

Rivkin, Allen and Laura Kerr
Doubleday & Co., Inc., Presents the Rivkin-Kerr Production of Hello Hollywood! A Book about the Movies by the People Who Make Them
N.Y.: Doubleday, 1962

Robinson, David
Buster Keaton
Bloomington, Ind.: Ind. U. Press, 1969

Robinson, David
The Great Funnies
N.Y.: Dutton, 1969

Robyns, Gwen
Light of a Star: The Career of Vivian Leigh
N.Y.: Barnes, 1970

Rodker, Francis
A Day with the Film Makers
London: Pitman, 1952

Rogers, Betty
Will Rogers
Garden City, N.Y.: Garden City Pub. Co., 1943

Rogers, Dale E.
Dale
Old Tappan, N.J.: Revell, Fleming H., 1971

Rooney, Mickey
I.E., An Autobiography
N.Y.: G.P. Putnam's Sons, 1965

Rosenbaum, J. (ed.)
Film Masters: An Anthology of Criticism on Thirty-Two Film Directors
N.Y.: Grosset & Dunlap, 1971

Rosenberg, Bernard and Harry Silverstein
Real Tinsel: The Story of Hollywood Told by the Men and Women Who Lived It
N.Y.: Macmillan, 1970

Rosenstein, Jaik
Hollywood Leg Man
L.A.: Madison Press, 1950

Roth, Lillian
Beyond My Worth
N.Y.: F. Fell, 1958

Roth, Lillian
I'll Cry Tomorrow
N.Y.: F. Fell, 1954

Roud, Richard
An Index: Max Ophuls
London: British Film Inst., 1958

Roud, Richard
Jean-Luc Godard
Garden City, N.Y.: Doubleday, 1968

Ruddy, Jonah and Jonathan Hill
The Bogey Man: Portrait of a Legend
London: Souvenir Press, 1965

Salachas, Gilbert
Federico Fellini: An Investigation into His Films and Philosophy
N.Y.: Crown, 1969

Samuels, C.
King: A Biography of Clark Gable
N.Y.: Popular Lib.,

Sarris, Andrew
The Films of Josef von Sternberg
N.Y.: Museum of Modern Art, 1966

Sarris, Andrew
Interviews with Film Directors
Indianapolis: Bobbs-Merrill, 1967

Schary, Dore
For Special Occasions
N.Y.: Random House, 1962

Schickel, Richard
The Disney Version
N.Y.: Avon, 1968

Schickel, Richard and Allen Hurlburt
The Stars: The Personalities Who Made the Movies
N.Y.: Dial Press, 1962

Scott, Audrey
I Was a Hollywood Stunt Girl
Philadelphia: Dorrance, 1969

Seib, Kenneth
James Agee: Promise and Fulfillment
Pittsburgh: U. of Pittsburgh Press, 1968

Sennett, Mack
King of Comedy
Garden City, N.Y.: Doubleday, 1954

Seton, Marie
Portrait of a Director
Bloomington, Ind.: Ind. U. Press, 1970

Seton, Marie
Sergei M. Eisenstein
N.Y.: Grove, 1969

Shaw, Arnold
Belafonte, An Unauthorized Biography
Philadelphia: Chilton, 1960

Shaw, Arnold
Sinatra: Twentieth-Century Romantic
N.Y.: Holt, Rinehart & Winston, 1968

Shelley, Frank
Stage and Screen
London: Pendulum Pubs., 1946

Sherman, Eric and Martin Rubin (eds.)
Director's Event: Interviews with Five American Film-Makers
N.Y.: Atheneum Pubs., 1969

Shipman, D.
Great Movie Stars: The Golden Years
N.Y.: Crown, 1970

Shulman, Irving
Harlow, An Intimate Biography
N.Y.: B. Geis Associates, 1964

Shulman, Irving
Valentino
N.Y.: Pocket Bks., 1968

Sieben, Pearl
The Immortal Jolson: His Life and Times
N.Y.: F. Fell, 1962

Sinclair, Upton
Upton Sinclair Presents William Fox
N.Y.: Arno, 1970 (rp.)

Singer, Kurt
The Danny Kaye Story
N.Y.: T. Nelson, 1958

Singer, Kurt
The Laughton Story: An Intimate Story of Charles Laughton
Philadelphia: Winston, 1954

Skolsky, Sidney
Time Square Tintypes
N.Y.: I. Washburn, 1930

Slezak, Walter
What Time's the Next Swan?
Garden City, N.Y.: Doubleday, 1962

Smith, George H.
Who Is Ronald Reagan?
N.Y.: Pyramid Pubs.,

Smith, Harry A.
Low Man on a Totem Pole
Garden City, N.Y.: Doubleday, Doran, 1941

Smith, J. M.
Jean Vigo
N.Y.: Praeger, 1971

Snyder, Robert L.
Pare Lorentz and the Documentary Film
Norman, Okla.: U. of Okla. Press, 1968

Solmi, Angelo
Fellini
London: Merlin Press, 1967

Sprigge, Elizabeth and Jean-Jacques Kihm
Jean Cocteau: The Man and the Mirror
N.Y.: Coward-McCann, 1968

Springer, John
The Fondas: The Films and Careers of Henry, Jane and Peter Fonda
N.Y.: Citadel, 1970

Stack, Oswald (ed.)
Pasolini on Pasolini
Bloomington, Ind.: Ind. U. Press, 1969

Steegmuller, Francis
Cocteau
Boston: Little, Brown, 1970

Steene, Birgitta
Ingmar Bergman
N.Y.: Twayne Pubs., 1968

Steiger, B. and C. Mank
Valentino: An Intimate and Shocking Expose
N.Y.: Macfadden-Bartell Corp.,

Steiger, Brad
Judy Garland
N.Y.: Ace, 1969

von Sternberg, Josef
Fun in a Chinese Laundry
N.Y.: Macmillan, 1965

Stuart, Ray
Immortals of the Screen
L.A.: Sherbourne Press, 1965

Sussex, Elisabeth
Lindsay Anderson
N.Y.: Praeger, 1969

Swindell, Larry
Spencer Tracy: A Biography
Cleveland: World Pub. Co., 1969

Swope, John
Camera over Hollywood
N.Y.: Random House, 1939

Sylvia (pseud.)
Hollywood Undressed
N.Y.: Brentano's, 1931

Tabori, Paul
Alexander Korda
London: Oldbourne, 1959

Talmey, Allene
Doug and Mary and Others
N.Y.: Macy-Masius, 1927

Taylor, Dwight
Joy Ride
N.Y.: G.P. Putnam's Sons, 1959

Taylor, Elizabeth
Elizabeth Taylor: An Informal Memoir
N.Y.: Harper & Row, 1965

Taylor, John R.
Cinema Eye, Cinema Ear: Some Key Film-Makers of the Sixties
N.Y.: Hill & Wang, 1964

Taylor, Robert L.
W. C. Fields: His Follies and Fortunes
Garden City, N.Y.: Doubleday, 1949

Taylor, Theodore
People Who Make Movies
Garden City, N.Y.: Doubleday, 1967

Thomas, B.
Heart of Hollywood
L.A.: Price, Stern & Sloan, 1971

Thomas, Bob
King Cohn
N.Y.: G. P. Putnam's Sons, 1967

Thomas, Bob
Selznick
Garden City, N.Y.: Doubleday, 1970

Thomas, Bob
Thalberg: Life and Legend
Garden City, N.Y.: Doubleday, 1969

Thomas, Bob
Walt Disney, the Art of Animation: The Story of the Disney Studio's Contribution to a New Art
N.Y.: Simon & Schuster, 1958

Thomas, Bob
Walt Disney: Magician of the Movies
N.Y.: Grosset & Dunlap,

Thomas, T.
Focus on Peter Ustinov
Cranbury, N.J.: Barnes, 1971

Thomas, T. T.
I, James Dean: The Real Story behind America's Most Popular Idol
N.Y.: Popular Lib., 1957

Thomas, Tony, Ruby Behlmer and Clifford McCarty
The Films of Errol Flynn
N.Y.: Citadel, 1969

Tomkies, M.
Duke: The Story of John Wayne
Chicago: Regnery, Henry, 1971

Torme, Mel
Other Side of the Rainbow: With Judy Garland on the Dawn Patrol
N.Y.: Wm. Morrow, 1970

Towers, Harry A.
Show Business: Stars of the World of Show Business
London: Low Marston, 1949

Trent, Spi M.
My Cousin Will Rogers
N.Y.: G. P. Putnam's Sons, 1939

Trotta, Vincent and Cliff Lewis
Screen Personalities
N.Y.: Grosset & Dunlap, 1933

Truffaut, Francois
Hitchcock
N.Y.: Simon & Schuster, 1967

Tullius, F. P.
Out of the Death Bag in West Hollywood
N.Y.: Macmillan, 1971

Twomey, Alfred E. and Arthur F. McClure
The Versatiles: A Study of Supporting Character Actors and Actresses in the American Motion Picture, 1930-1955
N.Y.: Barnes, 1969

Tyler, Parker
Chaplin, Last of the Clowns
N.Y.: Vanguard, 1948

Tynan, Kenneth
Alec Guinness
N.Y.: Macmillan, 1954

Tynan, Kenneth
Tynan Right and Left: Plays, Films, People, Places and Events
N.Y.: Atheneum Pubs., 1968

Von Ulm, Gerith
Charlie Chaplin, King of Tragedy
Naldwell, Ida.: Caxton Printers, 1940

Upson, Wilfrid
Movies and Monasteries in U.S.A.
Gloucester, England: Prinknash Abbey, 1950

Valentino, Rudolph
Reflections
Chicago: Champlin Law Printing Co., 1923

Vidor, King
A Tree Is a Tree
N.Y.: Harcourt, Brace & Winston, 1953

Wagenknecht, Edward
As Far as Yesterday: Memories and Reflections
Norman, Okla.: U. of Okla. Press, 1968

Wagenknecht, Edward (ed.)
Marilyn Monroe: A Composite View
Philadelphia: Chilton, 1969

Wagner, Robert L.
Film Folk
N.Y.: Century Co., 1918

Walker, Alexander
Stanley Kubrick Directs
N.Y.: Harcourt Brace Jovanovitch, 1971

Walker, Alexander
Stardom
N.Y.: Stein & Day, 1970

Walker, Stanley
Mrs. Astor's Horse
N.Y.: Frederick A. Stokes, 1935

Wanger, Walter and Joe Hyams
My Life with Cleopatra
N.Y.: Bantam Bks., 1963

Ward, John
Alain Resnais: Or The Theme of
 Time
Garden City, N.Y.: Doubleday,
 1968

Warner, Jack L.
My First Hundred Years in Hollywood
N.Y.: Random House, 1964,
 1965

Waterbury, Ruth
Elizabeth Taylor
N.Y.: Popular Lib., 1964

Weatherwax, Rudd B. and John
 H. Rothwell
The Story of Lassie
N.Y.: Duell, Sloan & Pearce,
 1950

Weegee (pseud.) and Mel Harris
Naked Hollywood
N.Y.: Pellegrini & Cudahy,
 1953

Weinberg, Herman G.
Josef von Sternberg
N.Y.: Dutton, 1967

Weinberg, Herman G.
The Lubitsch Touch: A Critical
 Study
N.Y.: Dutton, 1968

Weltman, Manuel & Raymond
 Lee
Pearl White: The Peerless Fear-
 less Girl
N.Y.: Barnes, 1969

West, Mae
Goodness Had Nothing to Do with
 It
Englewood Cliffs, N.J.:
 Prentice-Hall, 1959

West, Mae
The Wit and Wisdom of Mae
 West
N.Y.: Avon, 1967

White, Pearl
Just Me
N.Y.: George H. Doran, 1919

Wilcox, Herbert
Twenty-Five Thousand Sunsets:
 The Autobiography of Herbert
 Wilcox
N.Y.: Barnes, 1969

Williamson, Alice M.
Alice in Movieland
N.Y.: D. Appleton, 1928

Wilson, E.
The Show Business Nobody Knows
N.Y.: Cowles Bk. Co., 1971

Winchester, Clarence
An Innocent in Hollywood
London: Cassell, 1934

Windeler, Robert
Julie Andrews: A Biography
N.Y.: G.P. Putnam's Sons,
 1970

Wood, Alan
Mr. Rank: A Study of J. Arthur
 Rank and British Films
London: Hodder & Stoughton,
 1952

Wood, Robert
Crashing Hollywood
L.A.: Hollywood Imprint, 1952

Wood, Robin
Arthur Penn
N.Y.: Praeger, 1970

Wood, Robin
Hitchcock's Films
N.Y.: Barnes, 1965

Wood, Robin
Howard Hawks
Garden City, N.Y.: Doubleday, 1968

Wood, Robin
Ingmar Bergman
N.Y.: Praeger, 1969

Wood, Robin and Michael Walker
Claude Chabrol
N.Y.: Praeger, 1970

Wood, Tom
The Bright Side of Billy Wilder, Primarily
Garden City, N.Y.: Doubleday, 1970

Woollcott, Alexander
Enchanted Aisles
N.Y.: G.P. Putnam's Sons, 1924

Woollcott, Alexander
While Rome Burns
N.Y.: Viking, 1934

Young, Loretta
The Things I Had to Learn
Indianapolis: Bobbs-Merrill, 1961

Zavattini, Cesare and William Weaver
Zavattini: Sequences from a Cinematic Life
Englewood Cliffs, N.J.: Prentice-Hall, 1970

Zierold, Norman J.
The Child Stars
London: Macdonald, 1966

Zierold, Norman J.
Garbo
N.Y.: Stein & Day, 1969

Zierold, Norman J.
The Moguls
N.Y.: Coward-McCann, 1969

Zimmer, Jill Schary
With a Cast of Thousands: A Hollywood Childhood
N.Y.: Stein & Day, 1963

Zimmerman, Paul D. and Burt Goldblatt
The Marx Brothers and the Movies
N.Y.: G.P. Putnam's Sons, 1968

Zolotov, Maurice
It Takes All Kinds
N.Y.: Random House, 1952

Zolotov, Maurice
Marilyn Monroe
N.Y.: Harcourt, Brace & Co., 1960

Zukor, Adolph and Dale Kramer
The Public Is Never Wrong
N.Y.: G.P. Putnam's Sons, 1953

CATEGORY 10: FILM EDUCATION

Adam, Thomas R.
Motion Pictures in Adult Education
N. Y.: American Assn. for Adult Education, 1940

Allen, Don
The Electric Humanities
Dayton: Pflaum, 1971

Allen, Kenneth
Exploring the Cinema
London: Odhams Press, 1968

Amelio, Ralph J.
Film in the Classroom
Dayton: Pflaum, 1971

Amelio, Ralph J., Anita Owen and Susan Schaefer
Willowbrook Cinema Study Project
Dayton: Pflaum, 1969

American Association of Industrial Management
Film Guide for Industrial Training
N. Y.: Research Service, 1969

Andersen, Yvonne
Make Your Own Animated Movies
Boston: Little, Brown, 1970
(Grades 4 and up)

Andersen, Yvonne
Teaching Film Animation to Children
N. Y.: Van Nostrand Reinhold, 1970

Arnspiger, Varney C.
Measuring the Effectiveness of Sound Pictures as Teaching Aids
N. Y.: Teachers College, Columbia U., 1933

Batcheller, David R. (ed.)
Films for Use in Teaching Drama and Theatre
Washington, D. C.: American Educational Theatre Assn.,

Bauchard, Philippe
The Child Audience, a Report on Press, Film and Radio for Children
Paris: UNESCO, 1952

Becker, Samuel L.
The Relationships of Interest and Attention to Retention and Attitude Change
Iowa City, Ia.: U. of Ia., 1963

Bell, Geoffrey
8mm Film for Adult Audiences
Paris: UNESCO, 1968

Bernhard, Frederica and Elizabeth H. Flory
Educational Films in Sports
N.Y.: American Film Center, 1950

Bollman, Gladys and Henry Bollman
Motion Pictures for Community Needs
N.Y.: H. Holt, 1922

Boutwell, William (ed.)
Using Mass Media in the Classroom
N.Y.: Appleton-Century-Crofts, 1962

British Film Institute
Film Appreciation and Visual Education
London: British Film Inst., 1944

British Film Institite
Geography Teaching Films
London: British Film Inst., 1948

British Industrial and Scientific Film Association
Guide to Films on Education
London: British Industrial and Scientific Film Assn., 1969

British Universities' Film Council
Film and the Historian
London: British Universities' Film Council, 1968

British Universities' Film Council
Films for Universities
London: British Universities' Film Council, 1968

Brunstetter, Max R.
How to Use the Educational Sound Film
Chicago: U. of Chicago Press, 1937

Buchanan, Andrew
The Film in Education
London: Phoenix House, 1951

Buchanan, Andrew
Going to the Cinema
N.Y.: International Publications Service, 1970
(Grades 9 and up)

Capote, Truman, Eleanor Perry and Frank Perry
Trilogy: An Experiment in Multi-Media
N.Y.: Macmillan, 1969

Chamberlin, Frederick M. (ed.)
You and the Movies
Melbourne: Young Catholic Students' Movement, 1952

Chapman, William M. (ed.)
Films on Art
Kingsport, Tenn.: Kingsport Press, 1952

Colman, Hila
Making Movies: Student Films to Features
N.Y.: World Pub. Co., 1969
(Grades 7 and up)

Contemporary Film (Youth World Series)
N.Y.: Assn. Press, 1970

Cushing, Jane
One Hundred One Films for Character Growth
Notre Dame, Ind.: Fides Pubs., 1970

Dale, Edgar, Fannie W. Dunn, Charles F. Hoban, Jr. and Etta Schneider
Motion Pictures in Education: A Summary of the Literature
N.Y.: Arno, 1970 (rp.)

Dench, Ernest A.
Motion Picture Education
Cincinnati: Standard Pub. Co., 1917

Denny, Earl W.
A Study of the Effectiveness of Selected Motion Pictures for Reducing Frustration in Children
Ann Arbor, Mich.: Univ. Microfilms, 1959

Densham, D. H.
The Construction of Research Films
N.Y.: Pergamon, 1959

Devereux, Frederick L. et al
The Educational Talking Picture
Chicago: U. of Chicago Press, 1935

Educational Film Guide
N.Y.: H. W. Wilson,

Educational Policies Commission
Mass Communications and Education
Washington, D.C.: National Education Assn., 1958

Elliott, Godfrey M. (ed.)
Film and Education
N.Y.: Philosophical Lib., 1948

Ellis, Don C. and Laura Thornborough
Motion Pictures in Education
N.Y.: Thomas Y. Crowell, 1923

Everson, William K.
The American Movie
N.Y.: Atheneum Pubs., 1963
(Grades 7-10)

Farmer, Ronald J.
The Effect of Selected Film Sequences on Individuals toward Nature and Art Forms
Ann Arbor, Mich.: Univ. Microfilms, 1959

Fattu, Nicholas A. and Beryl B. Blain
Selected Films for Teacher Education
Bloomington, Ind.: Ind. U., 1950

Fearing, Franklin
Motion Pictures as a Medium of Instruction and Communication
Berkeley: U. of Cal. Press, 1950

Fensch, Thomas
Films on the Campus
Cranbury, N.J.: Barnes, 1970

Harriman, Byron L.
Influence of Group-Centered Therapy and Mental Health Films on Attitudes of Prisoners
Ann Arbor, Mich.: Univ. Microfilms, 1956

Herman, Lewis
Educational Films: Writing, Directing and Producing for Classroom, Television and Industry
Cleveland: World Pub. Co., 1965

Heyer, Robert and Anthony Meyer
Discovery in Film
Westminster, Md.: Paulist Press, 1969
(High School)

Hincks, Linda (ed.)
Films to Challenge You
Washington, D.C.: Division of Campus Ministry, 1969

Hoban, Charles F., Jr. and Edward B. Van Ormer
Instructional Film Research 1918-1950
N.Y.: Arno, 1970 (rp.)

Hodgkinson, Anthony W.
Screen Education: Teaching a Critical Approach to Cinema and Television
Paris: UNESCO, 1964

Hollis, Andrew P.
Motion Pictures for Instruction
N.Y.: Century Co, 1926

Hollis, Andrew P.
Value of "Movies" and "Talkies" in Education
Chicago: Herman A. DeVry, 1937

Hornberger, Theodor
Films for Teaching European Geography
Strasbourg: Council for Cultural Co-operation, Council of Europe, 1968

Janes, Hugh P.
Screen and Projector in Christian Education
Philadelphia: Westminster Press, 1932

Jennings, Gary
The Movie Book
N.Y.: Dial Press, 1963
(Grades 6 and up)

Jinks, W.
Celluloid Literature: Film in the Humanities
N.Y.: Glencoe Press, 1971

Kemp, Jerrold E. and others
Planning and Producing Audio-Visual Material
San Francisco: Chandler Pubs., 1967

Kitses, James
Talking about the Cinema
London: British Film Inst., 1966

Knowlton, D.C. and J.W. Tilton
Motion Pictures in History Teaching
New Haven, Conn.: Yale U. Press, 1929

Fern, George and E. B. Robbins
Teaching with Films
Milwaukee: Bruce Pub. Co., 1946

Feyen, Sharon and Donald Wigal
Screen Experiences: An Approach to Film
Dayton: Pflaum, 1969

Field, Mary and M. Miller
Boys' and Girls' Book of Films and Television
N.Y.: Roy Pubs.,
(Grades 6-10)

Film Centre, London
The Use of Mobile Cinema and Radio Vans in Fundamental Education
Paris: UNESCO, 1949

Films for Music Education and Opera Films: An International Selective Catalogue
Paris: UNESCO, 1962

Films on the Theatre and the Art of Pantomime
Paris: UNESCO, 1965

Forsdale, Louis (ed.)
8mm Sound Film and Education
N.Y.: Teachers College, Columbia U., 1962

Fritz, John O.
Film Persuasion in Education and Social Controversies: A Theoretical Analysis of the Components Manifest in Viewer-Film Involvement as They Affect the Viewer's Urge to Further Inquiry into Social Controversies
Ann Arbor, Mich.: U. Microfilms, 1957

George, William H.
The Cinema in School
London: I. Pitman & Sons, 1935

Giannetti, Louis D.
Understanding Movies
Englewood Cliffs, N.J.: Prentice-Hall, 1972

Goldman, Frederick and Linda R. Burnett
Need Johnny Read?
Dayton: Pflaum, 1971

Goldstein, Naomi Slutzky
The Effect of Animated Cartoons on Hostility in Children
Ann Arbor, Mich.: Univ. Microfilms, 1957

Goodman, Louis S.
Films for Personnel Management
N.Y.: Educational Film Lib. Assn.,

Groves, Peter D. (ed.)
Film in Higher Education and Research
Oxford, N.Y.: Pergamon, 1966

Hammontree, Marie
Walt Disney: Young Movie Maker
Indianapolis: Bobbs-Merrill,

Harcourt, Peter and Peter Theobald (eds.)
Film Making in Schools and Colleges
London: British Film Inst., 1966

Kuhns, William
Short Films in Religious Education
Dayton: Pflaum, 1967

Kuhns, William
Themes, Short Films for Discussion
Dayton: Pflaum, 1968

Kuhns, William and Robert Stanley
Behind the Camera: Filmmaking for Students
Dayton: Pflaum, 1970

Kuhns, William and Robert Stanley
Exploring the Film
Dayton: Pflaum, 1968

Lacey, Richard A.
Seeing with Feeling: Film in the Classroom
Philadelphia: W. B. Saunders, 1972

Laine, Elizabeth
Motion Pictures and Radio: Modern Techniques for Education
N. Y.: McGraw-Hill, 1938

Larsen, Rodger, Jr.
A Guide for Film Teachers to Filmmaking by Teenagers
N. Y.: Dept. of Cultural Affairs, 1968

Lauwerys, Joseph A. (ed.)
The Film in the School
London: Christophers, 1935

Lidstone, John and Don McIntosh
Children as Film Makers
N. Y.: Van Nostrand Reinhold, 1970

Limbacher, James L.
Using Films: A Handbook for the Program Planner
N. Y.: Educational Film Lib. Assn., 1967

Lowndes, Douglas
Film Making in Schools
N. Y.: Watson-Gupthill Pubs., 1968

MacCann, Richard D. (ed.)
Film and Society
N. Y.: C. Scribner's Sons, 1964

Maddux, Rachel, Stirling Silliphant and Neil D. Isaacs
Fiction into Film: A Walk in the Spring Rain
Knoxville, Tenn.: U. of Tenn. Press, 1970

Mallery, David
Film in the Life of the School: Programs, Practices, and New Directions
Boston: National Assn. of Independent Schools, 1968

Mallery, David
The School and the Art of Motion Pictures: A Challenge to Teachers
Boston: National Assn. of Independent Schools, 1966

Manchel, Frank
Cameras West
Englewood Cliffs, N. J.: Prentice-Hall, 1971

Manchel, Frank
Movies and How They Are Made
Englewood Cliffs, N. J.:
  Prentice-Hall, 1968

Manchel, Frank
When Movies Began to Move
Englewood Cliffs, N. J.:
  Prentice-Hall, 1969
(Grades 7 and up)

Manchel, Frank
When Movies Began to Speak
Englewood Cliffs, N. J.:
  Prentice-Hall, 1969
(Grades 7 and up)

Manvell, Roger
Shakespeare and the Film
N. Y.: Praeger, 1971

Marcus, F. H.
Film from Literature: Contrasts
  in Media
San Francisco: Chandler Pubs.,
  1971

May, Mark A. and Arthur A.
  Lumsdaine
Learning from Films
New Haven, Conn.: Yale U.
  Press, 1958

McCaffrey, Patrick J.
A Guide to Short Films for Religious Education
South Bend, Ind.: Fides Press,
  1967

McCaffrey, Patrick J.
A Guide to Short Films for Religious Education II
South Bend, Ind.: Fides Press,
  1968

Metcalfe, Lyne S. and H. G.
  Christensen
How to Use Talking Pictures in
  Business
N. Y.: Harper & Bros., 1938

Michaelis, Anthony R.
Research Films in Biology, Anthropology, Psychology and
  Medicine
N. Y.: Academic Press, 1955

Minney, Rubeigh J.
The Film-Maker and His World:
  A Young Person's Guide
London: Gollancz, 1964

Myers, R. R. and J. S. Long
Film-Forming Compositions
N. Y.: Dekker, Marcel, 1971

National Council for the Social
  Studies
How to Use a Motion Picture
Washington, D. C.: National Education Assn., 1965

National Education Association,
  Music Educators National Conference
Film Guide for Music Educators
Washington, D. C.: National Education Assn.,

Parker, Norton
Audiovisual Script Writing
New Brunswick, N. J.: Rutgers
  U. Press, 1968

Parrington, Ruth
An Educator's Guide to the Use of
  Film
Chicago: Argus Communications,
  1967

Peters, Jam M. L.
Teaching about the Film
Paris: UNESCO, 1961

Pfragner, Julius
Eye of History: The Motion Picture from Magic Lantern to Sound Film
Chicago: Rand McNally, 1964
(Grades 7 and up)

Rand, Helen and R. Lewis
Film and School
N.Y.: D. Appleton-Century, 1937

Reed, Kenneth A.
An Appraisal of the Usefulness of Films in Setting Time Standards by the Pace Method of Performance Rating
Ann Arbor, Mich.: Univ. Microfilms, 1958

Richardson, Alex
Screen Education for Schools
London: Schoolmaster Pub. Co., 1967

Richardson, Robert
Literature and Film
Bloomington, Ind.: Ind. U. Press, 1969

Roshal, Sol M.
Effects of Learner Representation in Film Mediated Perceptual Motor Learning
Port Washington, N.Y.: Office of Naval Research, 1949

Rulon, P. J.
Sound Motion Picture in Science Teaching
N.Y.: Johnson Reprint Co., (rp.)

Rynew, Arden
Filmmaking for Children
Dayton: Pflaum, 1971

Sarris, Andrew
The Film
Indianapolis: Bobbs-Merrill, 1968

Scheuer, Steven and John Culkin, S.J.
How to Study a Movie: An Introductory Guide to the Art of Motion Pictures
N.Y.: Dell Pub. Co., 1969

Schillaci, Anthony and John Culkin, S.J.
Films Deliver: Teaching Creatively with Film
N.Y.: Citation Press, 1970

Scollon, Robert W.
A Study of Some Communicator Variables Related to Attitude Restructuring through Motion Picture Films
Ann Arbor, Mich.: Univ. Microfilms, 1957

Sheridan, Marion C., Harold H. Owen, Jr., Ken Macrorie and Fred Marcus
The Motion Picture and the Teaching of English
N.Y.: Appleton-Century-Crofts, 1965

Slattery, Jamesetta
An Appraisal of the Effectiveness of Selected Instructional Sound Motion Pictures and Silent Filmstrips in Elementary School Instruction
Washington, D.C.: Catholic U. of America Press, 1953

Smith, Kinsley R. and E. B. van Ormer
Learning Theories and Instructional Film Research
Port Washington, N.Y.: Office of Naval Research, 1949

Smith, Richard
The Loop Film: A Practical Manual for Teachers, Sports Coaches, Research Workers, and Managers in Industry
London: Current Affairs, 1953

Sohn, David
Film Study and the English Teacher
Bloomington, Ind.: Ind. U. Press, 1966

Sohn, David
Film: The Creative Eye
Dayton: Pflaum, 1970

Steele, Robert S.
The Cataloging and Classification of Cinema Literature
Metuchen, N.J.: Scarecrow Press, 1967

Stein, Elisabeth M.
An Exploratory Investigation of the Use of Motion Pictures in the Treatment of Hospitalized Psychiatric Patients
Ann Arbor, Mich.: Univ. Microfilms, 1955

Steward, David D. (ed.)
Film Study in Higher Education
Washington, D.C.: American Council on Education, 1966

Storck, Henri
The Entertainment Film for Juvenile Audiences
Paris: UNESCO, 1950

Stork, Leopold
Industrial and Business Films: A Modern Means of Communication
London: Phoenix House, 1962

Sullivan, Bede
Movies, the Universal Language
South Bend, Ind.: Fides Press, 1967

Sweeting, Charles H. (ed.)
A Film Course Manual
Berkeley, Cal.: McCutchan Pub. Corp., 1970

Tiemens, Robert K.
The Comparative Effectiveness of Sound Motion Pictures and Printed Communications for the Motivation of High School Students in Mathematics
Iowa City, Ia.: Ste. U. of Ia., 1962

Whannel, Paddy
Studies in the Teaching of Film within Formal Education
London: British Film Inst., 1968

Whannel, Paddy and Peter Harcourt (eds.)
Film Teaching
London: British Film Inst., 1964

Wickham, Glynne (ed.)
The Relation between Universities and Films, Radio and Television
London: Butterworths Scientific Pubs., 1956

Wise, Harry A.
Motion Pictures as an Aid in Teaching American History
New Haven, Conn.: Yale U. Press, 1939

Wollenberg, Hans H.
Anatomy of the Film: An Illustrated Guide to Film Appreciation Based on a Course of Cambridge University Extension Lectures
London: Marsland Pubs., 1947

Wood, Benjamin D. and Frank N. Freeman
Motion Pictures in the Classroom
Boston: Houghton Mifflin, 1929

Wrigley, M. Jackson
The Film: Its Use in Popular Education
N.Y.: H. W. Wilson, 1922

CATEGORY 11: FILM-RELATED WORKS

Abbey, Merrill R.
Man, Media and the Message
N.Y.: Friendship Press, 1970

Achard, Paul
A New Slant on America
N.Y.: Rand McNally, 1931

Arnheim, Rudolf
Visual Thinking
Berkeley: U. of Cal. Press, 1969

Barnouw, Erik
Mass Communication: Television, Radio, Film, Press
N.Y.: Rinehart, 1956

Barrett, Marvin
The Jazz Age
N.Y.: Putnam, 1959

Beaumont, Charles
Remember? Remember?
N.Y.: Macmillan, 1963

Churchill, Allen
Remember When
N.Y.: Golden Press, 1967

Day, Barry
The Message of Marshall McLuhan
London: Lintas, 1967

Dorfles, Gillo
Kitsch: The World of Bad Taste
N.Y.: Universe Bks., 1969

Dulles, Foster R.
America Learns to Play: A History of Popular Recreation 1607-1940
N.Y.: Appleton-Century Co., 1940

Emery, Edwin, Phillip H. Ault, and Warren K. Agee
Introduction to Mass Communications
N.Y.: Dodd, Mead, 1968

Fabre, Maurice
A History of Communications
N.Y.: Hawthorne Bks., 1963

Finkelstein, Sidney
Sense and Nonsense of McLuhan
N.Y.: New World Paperbacks, 1968

Fischer, Heinz-Dietrich and John C. Merrill
International Communication: Media-Channels-Functions
N.Y.: Hastings House, 1970

Ford, Corey
The Time of Laughter
Boston: Little, Brown, 1967

Franks, A. H.
Ballet for Film and Television
London: I. Pitman, 1950

Gordon, George N.
The Languages of Communication: A Logical and Psychological Examination
N.Y.: Hastings House, 1969

Gorelick, Mordecai
New Theatres for Old
N.Y.: Dutton, 1962

Gross, Martin A.
The Nostalgia Quiz Book
New Rochelle, N.Y.: Arlington House, 1970

Hall, James B. and Barry Ulanov
Modern Culture and the Arts
Hightstown, N.J.: McGraw-Hill, 1967

Hall, Stuart and Paddy Whannel
The Popular Arts
N.Y.: Pantheon Bks., 1965

Hancock, Ralph
Fabulous Boulevard
N.Y.: Funk & Wagnalls, 1949

Hill, Edwin C.
The American Scene
N.Y.: M. Witmark & Sons, 1933

Horan, James D.
The Desperate Years, a Pictorial History of the Thirties
N.Y.: Crown, 1962

Jacobs, Norman (ed.)
Culture for the Millions
Boston: Beacon, 1964

Kepes, Gyorgy (ed.)
The Visual Arts Today
Middletown, Conn.: Wesleyan U. Press, 1960

Kernodle, George R.
Invitation to the Theatre
N.Y.: Harcourt, Brace & World, 1967

Kostelanetz, Richard (ed.)
The New American Arts
N.Y.: Horizon, 1965

Lindey, Alexander
Plagiarism and Originality
N.Y.: Harper, 1952

Lynch, William F.
The Image Industries
N.Y.: Sheed & Ward, 1959

MacGowan, Kenneth
The Theatre of Tomorrow
N.Y.: Boni & Liveright, 1921

McLuhan, Herbert Marshall
Understanding Media: The Extensions of Man
N.Y.: McGraw-Hill, 1964

Morris, Lloyd R.
Not So Long Ago
N.Y.: Random House, 1949

Nye, Russel B.
The Unembarrassed Muse: The Popular Arts in America
N.Y.: Dial Press, 1970

Palmer, Arnold
Straphangers
London: Selwyn & Blount, 1927

Rosenberg, Bernard and David M. White (eds.)
Mass Culture: The Popular Arts in America
N.Y.: Macmillan, 1957

Ruesch, Jurgen and Weldon Kees
Non-Verbal Communication: Notes on the Visual Perception of Human Relations
Berkeley: U. of Cal. Press, 1956

Schramm, Wilbur L.
Communications in Modern Society
Urbana, Ill.: U. of Ill. Press, 1948

Schramm, Wilbur L. (ed.)
Mass Communications
Urbana, Ill.: U. of Ill. Press, 1949

Seldes, Gilbert V.
The New Mass Media--Challenge to a Free Society
Washington, D.C.: American Assn. of Univ. Women, 1968

Sontag, Susan
Against Interpretation and Other Essays
N.Y.: Farrar, Straus & Giroux, 1966

Sontag, Susan
Styles of Radical Will
N.Y.: Delta Bks., 1970

Stearn, Gerald E. (ed.)
McLuhan, Hot and Cool
N.Y.: Dial Press, 1967

Stearns, Harold E. (ed.)
America Now
N.Y.: C. Scribner's Sons, 1938

Steinberg, Charles S.
The Communicative Arts
N.Y.: Hastings House, 1970

Steinberg, Charles S.
Mass Media and Communication
N.Y.: Hastings House, 1966

Sutro, John (ed.)
Diversion: Twenty-Two Authors on the Lively Arts
London: Parrish, 1950

Thompson, Denys (ed.)
Discrimination and Popular Culture
Baltimore: Penguin, 1965

Wagner, Geoffrey A.
Parade of Pleasure: A Study of Popular Iconography in the U.S.A.
N.Y.: Lib. Pubs., 1955

White, David M. (ed.)
Pop Culture in America
Westminster, Md.: Quadrangle Bks., 1970

Whitney, Elwood (ed.)
Symbology, the Use of Symbols in Visual Communications
N.Y.: Hastings House, 1960

CATEGORY 12: CAREERS IN FILM

Barleben, Karl A.
Earning Money with Your Movie
 Camera
Philadelphia: Chilton, 1960

Denis, Paul
Your Career in Show Business
N.Y.: Dutton, 1948

Emerson, John and Anita Loos
Breaking into the Movies
N.Y.: James A. McCann, 1921

Gordon, George N. and Irving
 Falk
Your Career in Film Making
N.Y.: Julian Messner, 1969

Humfrey, Robert
Careers in the Films
London: I. Pitman, 1938

Hungerford, Mary J.
Dancing in Commercial Motion
 Pictures
N.Y.: Corner Bk. Shop, 1946

Joels, Merrill E.
How to Get into Show Business
N.Y.: Hastings House, 1969

Jones, Charles R. (ed.)
Breaking into the Movies
N.Y.: Unicorn Press, 1927

Jones, Charles R.
Your Career in Motion Pictures,
 Radio and Television
N.Y.: Sheridan House,

Kanigher, Robert
How to Make Money Writing for
 the Movies
N.Y.: Cambridge House, 1943

Lee, Norman
Money for Film Stories
London: I. Pitman, 1937

Moore, Dick
Opportunities in Acting: Stage,
 Motion Pictures, Television
N.Y.: Vocational Guidance Manuals, 1963

Photoplay Research Society
Opportunities in the Motion Picture Industry
N.Y.: Arno, 1970 (rp.)

Reed, Dena
Success Tips from Young Celebrities
N.Y.: Grosset & Dunlap, 1967

Reimherr, Herbert
Hollywood and Moving Pictures for
 Those Planning a Film Career
L.A.: David Graham Fischer, 1932

Shapiro, Clarence M.
I Scout for Movie Talent
Chicago: A. Kroch & Son, 1940

CATEGORY 13: BIBLIOGRAPHIES, GUIDES, AND INDEXES

Ackermann, Jean M.
Guide to Films on International Development
Beverly Hills: Film Sense, 1967

Alpert, Hollis and Andrew Sarris
Film 68/69
N.Y.: Simon & Schuster, 1969

American Film Institute (ed.)
American Film
N.Y.: R.R. Bowker, 1970

The American Film Institute Catalogue (Vol. 1: 1921-1930)
N.Y.: R.R. Bowker,

American Library Association Audio-Visual Committee
Films for Libraries
Chicago: American Lib. Assn., 1962

Baden, Anne L. (comp.)
Moving Pictures in the United States and Foreign Countries: A Selected List of Recent Writings
Washington, D.C.: U.S. Lib. of Congress, Div. of Bibliography, 1940

Baker, Frank A.
A Catalogued Technical Review of Motion Picture Activity within the United States, 1894-1896
Ann Arbor, Mich.: Univ. Microfilms, 1961

Bibliography of Film Librarianship
Zion, Ill.: International Scholarly Bk. Service,

Bibliography of Filmology as Related to the Social Sciences
Paris: UNESCO, 1954

Blum, Daniel C.
Screen World (10 Vols.)
N.Y.: Biblo & Tannen, 1969

Blum, Eleanor
Reference Books in the Mass Media: An Annotated, Selected Booklist Covering Book Publishing, Broadcasting, Films, Newspapers, Magazines, and Advertising
Urbana, Ill.: U. of Ill. Press, 1962

British Film Institute
Films in 1951
London: British Film Inst., 1951

Cameron, James R. (comp.)
Cameron's Encyclopedia on Sound
 Motion Pictures
Manhattan Beach, N.Y.:
 Cameron Pub. Co., 1930

Catalogue of French Ethnograph-
 ical Films
Paris: UNESCO, 1955

Christeson, Frances M.
A Guide to the Literature of the
 Motion Picture
Berkeley: U. of Cal. Press, 1938

Clason, W. E.
Elsevier's Dictionary of Cinema,
 Sound, and Music in Six Lan-
 guages
N.Y.: Elsevier Pub. Co., 1956

Cowie, Peter (ed.)
International Film Guide
N.Y.: Barnes, 1963

Cowie, Peter (ed.)
International Film Guide 1969
N.Y.: Barnes, 1969

Cowie, Peter (ed.)
International Film Guide 1970
N.Y.: Barnes, 1970

Cowie, Peter (ed.)
International Film Guide 1971
N.Y.: Barnes, 1971

Daisne, Johan
Dictionnaire Filmographique de
 la Litterature Mondiale, Film-
 ographic Dictionary of World
 Literature, Filmographisches
 Lexikon der Weltliteratur,
 Filmografisch Lexicon der
 Weredliteratur (Vol. 1)
N.Y.: Humanities Press, 1970

Dale, Edgar and John Morrison
Motion Picture Discrimination:
 An Annotated Bibliography
Columbus, Oh.: Oh. Ste. U.,
 195?

Denby, D. (ed.)
Film 70-71
N.Y.: Simon & Schuster, 1972

Dimmitt, Richard B.
Actor's Guide to the Talkies,
 1949-1964 (2 vols.)
Metuchen, N.J.: Scarecrow
 Press, 1967

Dimmitt, Richard B.
A Title Guide to the Talkies (2
 vols.)
N.Y.: Scarecrow Press, 1965

Enser, A. G. S.
Filmed Books and Plays
London: British Bk. Center, 1964

Festival Film Guides (11 vols.)
N.Y.: Educational Film Lib.
 Assn., 1959-1967

Film Daily Yearbook of Motion
 Pictures 1918-1969 (52 vols.)
N.Y.: Arno,

Film Daily Yearbook of Motion
  Pictures and Television 1970
N.Y.: Arno Press, 1970

The Film Index: A Bibliography
  Vol. 1
N.Y.: Arno, 1966 (rp.)

Film Library Association
Films: A Union Catalogue of
  16mm Motion Pictures
Seattle: Film Lib. Assn., 1951

Film Review Index 1970
Monterey Park, Cal.: Audio-
  Visual Associates,

Film Review Index 1971
Monterey Park, Cal.: Audio-
  Visual Associates,

Geltzer, George
An Index to the Silent American
  Serial, 1913-1930
N.Y.: New Theodore Huff
  Memorial Film Society, 1955

Graham, Peter
A Dictionary of the Cinema
N.Y.: Barnes, 1964

Helfand, Esther
Films for Young Adults
N.Y.: Educational Film Lib.
  Assn.,

Herring, Robert
Films of the Year 1927-1928
London: The Studio, 1928

Hoban, Charles F., Jr. and
  Edward B. Van Ormer
Instructional Film Research
  1918-1950
N.Y.: Arno, 1970 (rp.)

Jackson-Wrigley, M. and Eric
  Leyland
The Cinema, Historical, Techni-
  cal, and Bibliographical
London: Grafton & Co., 1939

Jones, Emily Strange
Films and People
N.Y.: Educational Film Lib.
  Assn., 1952

Jordan, Thurston C., Jr.
Glossary of Motion Picture Ter-
  minology
Menlo Park, Cal.: Pacific Coast
  Pub., 1968

Kennedy, P. (ed.)
Films on Traditional Music and
  Dance: A First International
  Catalogue
N.Y.: Unipub, 1970

Kitching, Jessie B. and Emily S.
  Jones
Index to Selected Film Lists
N.Y.: Educational Film Lib.
  Assn., 1950

Kone, Grace A.
The 8mm Film Directory
N.Y.: Educational Film Lib.
  Assn.,

Kula, Sam
Bibliography of Film Librarian-
  ship
London: Lib. Assn., 1967

Lavastida, Aubert
Motion Pictures Produced by
  Members of the University
  Film Producers Association
N.Y.: Educational Film Lib.
  Assn., 1954

Levitan, Eli
An Alphabetical Guide to Motion
   Pictures, Television, and Vid-
   eo Tape Production
N.Y.: McGraw-Hill, 1970

Library of Congress
Motion Pictures, 1894-1959 (4
   vols.)
Washington, D.C.: Lib. of
   Congress, 1951-1960

Library of Congress
National Union Catalogue
   1953-1957 Vol. 28: Motion Pic-
      tures and Film Strips
   1958-1962 Vols. 53, 54: Mo-
      tion Pictures and Film Strips
   1963-1967 Motion Pictures and
      Film Strips (2 vols.)
Ann Arbor, Mich.: J. W.
   Edwards,

Limbacher, James L. (ed.)
Feature Films on 8mm and 16mm:
   A Directory of Feature Films
   Available for Rental, Sale or
   Lease in the United States
N.Y.: R. R. Bowker, 1971

Limbacher, James L. (comp.)
Remakes, Series, and Sequels on
   Film and Television
Dearborn, Mich.: Dearborn
   Public Lib., 1969

Lloyd, Blodwen (ed.)
Science in Films: A World Re-
   view and Reference Book
London: S. Low Marston, 1948

Maltin, Leonard (ed.)
TV Movies
N.Y.: New American Lib., 1969

McCarty, Clifford
Film Composers in America, a
   Checklist of Their Work
Glendale, Cal.: J. Valentine,
   1953

Michael, Paul and James R.
   Parish (eds.)
American Movies Reference
   Book: The Sound Era
Englewood Cliffs, N.J.:
   Prentice-Hall, 1969

Miller, Maude M. (ed.)
Winchester's Screen Encyclope-
   dia
London: Winchester Pubs., 1948

Morgenstein, Joseph and Stefan
   Kanfer
Film 69/70
N.Y.: Simon & Schuster, 1970

Munden, Kenneth W. (ed.)
Feature Films 1921-1930
N.Y.: R. R. Bowker, 1970

National Information Center for
   Educational Media
NICEM Media Indexes (4 vols.)
   Vol. 1: Index to 16mm Educa-
      tional Film
   Vol. 2: Index to 8mm Educa-
      tional Motion Picture Car-
      tridges
   Vol. 4: Index to 35mm Educa-
      tional Films
N.Y.: R. R. Bowker,

Neusbaum, Frank S.
International Calendar of Film
   Festivals, Contests, Awards
Univ. Park, Pa.: Univ. Film
   Producers Assn., 1957

New York Public Library Staff
Films: 1969 Catalogue of the Film Collection in the New York Public Library
N.Y.: N.Y. Public Lib., 1969

Niver, Kemp R.
Motion Pictures from the Library of Congress Paper Print Collection, 1894-1912
Berkeley: U. of Cal. Press, 1967

Pickard, R. A.
Dictionary of One-Thousand Best Films
N.Y.: Assn. Press, 1971

Rebel, Enrique J.
Great Cameramen: An Annotated Dictionary
N.Y.: Barnes, 1969

Reid, Seerley
United States Government and Pan American Union Motion Pictures on the Other American Republics
Washington, D.C.: U.S. Govt. Printing Office, 1950

Reid, Seerley
U.S. Government Films for Public Educational Use
Washington, D.C.: U.S. Dept. of H.E.W., 1961

Reid, Seerley and Virginia Wilkins
3434 U.S. Government Films
Washington, D.C.: Office of Education, 1951

Salem, James M.
Guide to Critical Reviews, Pt. 4: The Screenplays
Metuchen, N.J.: Scarecrow Press, 1970

Scheuer, Steven H. (ed.)
Movies on T.V.
N.Y.: Bantam Bks., 1968

Schickel, Richard and John Simon (eds.)
Film 67/68
N.Y.: Simon & Schuster, 1968

Schuster, M. (ed.)
Motion Picture Performers: A Bibliography of Magazine and Periodical Articles 1960-1969
Metuchen, N.J.: Scarecrow Press, 1971

Selected List of Catalogues for Short Films and Filmstrips
Paris: UNESCO, 1964

Shinde, M. K. (ed.)
Shinde's Dictionary of Cine Art and Film Craft
Bombay: Popular Prakashan, 1962

Solomon, Martin B., Jr. and Nora G. Lovan
Annotated Bibliography of Films in Automation, Data Processing and Computer Science
Lexington, Ky.: Univ. Press of Ky., 1967

Speed, F. Maurice (ed.)
Film Review 1966-1968
N.Y.: Barnes, 1967

Speed, F. Maurice (ed.)
Film Review 1968-1969
N.Y.: Barnes, 1968

Speed, F. Maurice (ed.)
Film Review 1969-1970
N.Y.: Barnes, 1969

Speed, F. Maurice (ed.)
Film Review 1971-1972
Cranbury, N.J.: Barnes, 1971

Sprecher, Daniel (ed.)
Guide to Films about Famous
 People: 16mm
Alexandria, Va.: Serina Press,
 1969

Sprecher, Daniel (ed.)
Guide to State Loan Film
Alexandria, Va.: Serina Press,
 1969

Telberg, Val
Russian-English Dictionary of
 Science, Technology and Art
 of Cinematography
N.Y.: Telberg Bk. Co., 1961

Ten Years of Films on Art:
 1952-1962
 Vol. 1: Paintings and Sculpture
Paris: UNESCO, 1966

Ten Years of Films on Ballet and
 Classical Dance, 1956-1965
Paris: UNESCO, 1968

Thompson, Howard
New York Times Guide to Movies
 on T.V.
Westminster, Md.: Quadrangle
 Bks., 1970

Townsend, Derek
Photography and Cinematography
London: A. Redman, 1964

Vincent, Carl
General Bibliography of Motion
 Pictures
Rome: Edizioni dell'Ateneo,
 1953

Walls, Howard L.
Motion Pictures, 1894-1912,
 Identified from the Records of
 the United States Copyright Of-
 fice
Washington, D.C.: Lib. of
 Congress, 1953

Weaver, John T. (comp.)
Forty Years of Screen Credits
 1929-1969
Metuchen, N.J.: Scarecrow
 Press, 1970

Weaver, John T.
Twenty Years of Silents
Metuchen, N.J.: Scarecrow
 Press, 1971

Weber, David
99+ Films on Drugs
N.Y.: Educational Film Lib.
 Assn.,

Williams, Tess M.
Directory of Non-Royalty Films
 for Television
Ames, Ia.: Ia. Ste. U. Press,
 1954

Willis, John (ed.)
Screen World
N.Y.: Crown, 1962 on

Winchester, Clarence (ed.)
The World Film Encyclopedia, a Universal Screen Guide
London: Amalgamated Press, 1933

World Film Directory
Paris: UNESCO, 1962

Wrigley, M. Jackson and Eric Leyland
The Cinema: Historical, Technical, and Bibliographical: A Survey for Librarians and Students
London: Grafton & Co., 1939

Zwerdling, S. (ed.)
Film and T.V. Festival World-Wide Directory
N.Y.: DBS Pubs., 1971

CATEGORY 14: SELECTED WORKS IN FOREIGN LANGUAGES

Agel, Henri
Le Cinéma
Tournai: Casterman, 1955

Agel, Henri
Le Cinéma a-t-il une Âme?
Paris: Éditions du Cerf, 1952

Agel, Henri
Le Cinéma et le Sacré
Paris: Éditions du Cerf, 1961

Agel, Henri
Esthétique du Cinéma
Paris: Presses Universitaires de France, 1957

Agel, Henri
Les Grands Cinéastes
Paris: Éditions Universitaires, 1959

Agel, Henri
Miroirs de l'Insolite dans le Cinéma Français
Paris: Éditions du Cerf, 1958

Agel, Henri
Le Prêtre à l'Écran
Paris: P. Tequi, 1953

Agel, Henri
Robert Bresson
Bruxelles: Club du Livre de Cinéma, 1957

Agel, Henri
Robert J. Flaherty, Preséntation par Henri Agel
Paris: Éditions Seghers, 1965

Agel, Henri
Romance Américaine
Paris: Éditions du Cerf, 1963

Agel, Henri
Vittorio de Sica
Paris: Éditions Universitaires, 1955

Agel, Henri
Le Western
Paris: Minard, 1961

Agel, Henri et al
Sept Ans de Cinéma Français
Paris: Éditions du Cerf, 1953

Agel, Henri and Geneviève Agel
Précis d'Initiation au Cinéma
Paris: Éditions de l'École, 1963

Agel, Henri and Geneviève Agel
Voyage dans le Cinéma
Tournai: Casterman, 1962

Albrecht, Gerd
*Film und Verkündigung:
   Probleme des Religiösen Films*
Gütersloh: C. Bertelsmann, 1962

Amberg, Friedrich G.
Werbung im Filmtheater
Berlin: Kulturbuch-Verlag, 1956

Amengual, Barthélemy
René Clair
Paris: Éditions Seghers, 1963

Angotti, Roaria
Osservazioni sul Cinema
Rome: Cinestudio ABC, 1943

Antonioni, Michelangelo
*Sei Film: Le Amiche, Il Grido,
   L'Avventura, La Notte,
   L'Eclisse, Deserto Rosso*
Torino: Einaudi, 1964

Aranda, Francisco
Cinema de Vanguardia en España
Lisboa: Guimarães, 1953

Aristarco, Guido (ed.)
*L'Arte del Film: Antologia
   Storico-Critica*
Milano: Bompiani, 1950

Aristarco, Guido
*Cinema Italiano 1960: Romanzo
   e Antiromanzo*
Milano: I. Saggiatore, 1961

Aristarco, Guido (ed.)
Miti e Realtà nel Cinema Italiano
Milano: I. Saggiatore, 1961

Aristarco, Guido (ed.)
Storia delle Teoriche del Film
Torino: G. Einaudi, 1951

Artaud, Antonin
Oeuvres Complètes
Paris: Gallimard, 1961

Artis, Pierre
*Histoire du Cinéma Américain,
   1926-47*
Paris: C. d'Halluin, 1947

Artis-Gener, A.
*La Escenografía en el Teatro y
   el Cine*
Mexico: Editorial Centauro, 1947

Auriol, Jean G. et al
Le Cinéma
Paris: Aux Éditions du Cynge, 1932

Ayfre, Amédée
Le Cinéma et la Foi Chrétienne
Paris: Fayard, 1960

Ayfre, Amédée
Conversion aux Images?
Paris: Éditions du Cerf, 1964

Ayfre, Amédée
*Dieu au Cinéma: Problemes
   Esthétiques du Film Religieux*
Paris: Presses Universitaires de
   France, 1953

Baechlin, Peter and Maurice
   Müller-Strauss
Le Presse Filmée dans le Monde
Paris: UNESCO, 1951

Bamberger, Stefan
Studenten und Film
Zürich: Alten, O. Walter, 1958

Bandini, Baldo
Ragionamenti sulla Scenografia
Milan: Poligno Societa Editrice, 1945

Barbaro, Umberto
Il Film e il Risarcimento Marxista Dell'arte
Roma: Editori Riuniti, 1960

Barbaro, Umberto
Poesia del Film
Roma: Edizioni Filmcritica, 1955

Batz, Jean C.
A Propos de la Crise de l'Industrie du Cinéma
Bruxelles: Université Libre de Bruxelles, 1963

Bazin, André
Qu'est-ce que le Cinéma?
Paris: Éditions du Cerf, 1958-1962 (4 vols.)

Becker, Raymond de
De Tom Mix à James Dean: ou, Le Mythe de l'Homme dans le Cinéma Américaine
Paris: A. Fayard, 1959

Benayoun, Robert
John Huston
Paris: Seghers, 1966

Benoit-Lévy, Jean
Les Grandes Missions du Cinéma
Montreal: L. Parizeau & Compagnie, 1945

Béranger, Jean
La Grande Aventure du Cinéma Suédois
Paris: E. Losfeld, 1960

Béranger, Jean
Ingmar Bergman et Ses Films
Paris: Le Terrain Vague, 1959

Béranger, Jean
Le Nouveau Cinéma Scandinave, de 1957 à 1968
Paris: Le Terrain Vague, 1968

Bessy, Maurice and Giuseppe Lo Duca
Georges Méliès, Mage et "Mes Memoires" par Méliès
Paris: Prisma, 1945

Beyer, Nils
En Bok Om Film
Stockholm: Radiojänst, 1949

Bianchi, Pietro
L'occhio del Cinema
Milano: Garzanti, 1957

Bianchi, Pietro and Franco Berutti
Storia del Cinema
Milano: Garzanti, 1957

Bizzarri, Libero
L'industria Cinematografica Italiana
Firenze: Parenti, 1958

Blanco, Armindo
Tempo de Cinema
Lisboa: Cosmos, 1956

Blasetti, Alessandro (ed.)
Cinema Italiano Oggi
Roma: C. Bestetti, 1952

Bode, Alolf W.
Das Kleine Film-Lexikon
Frankfurt: Humboldt-Verlag, 1954

Bondi, Brunello
Cinema e Realtà
Roma: Edizioni Cinque Lune, 1957

Borde, Raymond and André Bouissy
Le Néo-Réalisme Italien: Une Expérience de Cinéma Social
Lausanne: Clairefonaine, 1960

Bounoure, Gaston
Alain Resnais
Paris: Éditions Seghers, 1962

Boussinot, Roger
Le Cinéma est Mort, Vive le Cinéma?
Paris: les Lettres Nouvelles, Denoël, 1967

Bovay, Georges M. et al
Cinéma, un Oeil Ouvert sur le Monde
Lausanne: Le Guide du Livre, 1952

Brasil, Assis
Cinema e Literatura
Rio de Janeiro: Tempo Brasileiro, 1967

Broll, Gunter
Magie des Films
Munchen: Suddentscher Verlag, 1953

Brusendorff, Ove and Poul Malmkjaer
Erotick I Filmen
Kobenhavn: Thaning & Appels Forlag, 1965

Buñuel, Luis
Viridiana
Paris: Interspectacles, 1962

Calvino, Vittorio
Guida al Cinema
Milano: Nuova Accademia, 1954

Carpi, Fabio
Cinema Italiano del Dopoguerra
Milano: Schwartz, 1958

Carton, Pauline
Histories de Cinéma
Lausanne: J. Rollan, 1956

Castellani, Leandro
Temi e Figure del Cinema Contemporaneo
Roma: Editrice Studium, 1963

Cauliez, Armand J.
Le Film Criminel et le Film Policier
Paris: Éditions du Cerf, 1956

Cavallé, Mario
Tecnica delle Costruzioni di Cinema e Teatri
Milano: Gorlich, 1951

Cayrol, Jean
Muriel
Paris: Éditions du Seuil, 1963

Chabannes, Jacques
Les Coulisses du Cinéma
Paris: Hachette, 1959

Charensol, George et al
Le Cinéma
Paris: Larousse, 1966

Chauvet, Louis
Le Cinéma à Travers le Monde
Paris: Hachette, 1961

Chevalier, Jacques
Regards Neufs sur le Cinéma
Paris: Seuil, 1953

Chevalier, Louis
Cinéma et Civilisation
Paris: Le Cours de Droit, 1968

Chiarini, Luigi
Il Film nei Problemi Dell'arte
Roma: Ateneo, 1949

Chiarini, Luigi
Il Film Nella Battaglia delle Idee
Milano: Fratelli Bocca, 1954

Ciarletta, Nicola
Da Amleto a Charlot
Roma: Edizioni Filmcritica, 1954

Cocteau, Jean
La Belle et la Bête: Journal d'un Film
Monaco: Éditions du Rocher, 1958

Cocteau, Jean
Orphée: Film
Paris: La Parade, 1951

Cocteau, Jean
Le Sang d'un Poète
Monaco: Éditions du Rocher, 1957

Cohen-Séat, Gilbert
L'Action sur l'Homme: Cinéma et Télévision
Paris: Éditions Denoël, 1961

Cohen-Séat, Gilbert
Essai sur les Principes, d'une Philosophie du Cinéma
Paris: Presses Universitaires de France, 1958

Cohen-Séat, Gilbert
Problèms du Cinéma et de l'Information Visuelle
Paris: Presses Universitaires de France, 1959

Coissac, G. M.
Histoire du Cinématographe de ses Origines à nos Jours
Paris: Éditions du "Cinéopse," 1925

Colpi, Henri
Défense et Illustration de la Musique dans le Film
Lyon: Société d'Édition de Recherches et de Documentation Cinématographiques, 1963

Costa, Alves
Breve História de Imprensa Cinematográfica Portuguesa
Porto: Cine-club do Porto, 1954

Coursodon, Jean-Pierre and Yves Boisset
Vingt Ans de Cinéma Américain (1940-1960)
Paris: Éditions C. I. B., 1961

Covi, Antonio
La Critica Estetica del Film
Milano: Editrice Selecta, 1959

Curtis, Jean L.
Cinéma
Paris: Julliard, 1967

Daquin, Louis
Le Cinéma, Notre Métier
Paris: Les Éditeurs Français Réunis, 1960

Debrix, Jean
Les Fondements de l'Art Cinématographique
Paris: Éditions du Cerf, 1960

Deslandes, Jacques
Histoire Comparée du Cinéma: Volume 1
Paris: Casterman, 1966

Deslandes, Jacques and Jacques Richard
Histoire Comparée du Cinéma: Volume 2
Paris: Casterman, 1968

Le Développement des Moyens d'Information en Afrique (Presse, Radio, Film, Télévision)
Paris: UNESCO, 1962

Doorn, Bernardus J. van
De Film een Gevaar?
Den Haag: Landejik Bureau van de Katholieke Film Actie, 1956

Dorigo, Francesco
Civiltà e Cinema
Venezia: S. Marco, 1959

Dorrell, J. M.
Cine Italiano
Madrid: Brújula del Cine, 1952

Durand, Jacques
Le Cinéma et son Public
Paris: Sirey, 1958

Duras, Marguerite
Une Aussi Longue Absence
Paris: Gallimard, 1961

Duvillars, Pierre
Pin-up Femmes Fatales et Ingénues Libertines: L'érotisme au Cinéma
Paris: Éditions du xxe Siècle, 1951

Eberhardt, Konrad
Aktorzy Filmu Polskiego
Warszawa: Wydawn, 1962

L'éducation Cinématographique
Paris: UNESCO, 1961

Eisner, Lotte H.
L'Écran Démoniaque: Influence de Max Reinhardt et de l'Expressionisme
Paris: Éditions André Bonne, 1952

Eisner, Lotte H. (ed.)
Film, Rundfunk, Fernsehen
Frankfurt am Main: Fischer Bücherei, 1958

Epstein, Jean
Cinéma
Paris: Éditions de la Sirène, 1921

Epstein, Jean
Esprit du Cinéma
Genève: Jeheber, 1955

Esnault, Philippe
Chronologie du Cinéma Mondial des Origines à Nos Jours
Paris: Grands Films Classiques, 1963

Estève, Michel et al
Le Nouveau Cinéma Hongrois
Paris: Minard, 1969

Étude sur la Création de Centres Nationaux de Catalogage de Films et de Programmes de Télévision
Paris: UNESCO, 1963

Fallaci, Oriana
I Sette Peccati di Hollywood, Presentato da Orson Welles
Milano: Longanesi, 1958

Fellini, Federico and Tullio Pinelli
La Strada
Roma: Bianco e Nero, 1955

Fernández Cuenca, Carlos
Cine Religioso: Filmográfia Crítica
Valladolid: Sever-Cuesta, 1960

Fescourt, Henri
La Foi et les Montagnes; ou, Le Septième Art au Passé
Paris: P. Montel, 1960

Flory, Robert
La Lanterne Magique
Lausanne: Cinémathèque Suisse, 1966

Ford, Charles
Bréviaire du Cinéma: Soixante Ans de Pensée Cinégraphique
Paris: Éditions Publications, 1959

Ford, Charles
Caméra et "Mass Media:" La Civilisation à la l'Âge des Deux Écrans
Tours: Mame, 1970

Ford, Charles
Le Cinéma au Service de la Foi
Paris: Plon, 1953

Ford, Charles
Histoire Populaire du Cinéma
Tours: Mame, 1955

Forlani, Rémo
Cinéma, Télévision
Paris: Édicope, 1961

Fraenkel, Heinrich
Unsterblicher Film: Die Grosse Chronik von der Laterna Magica bis zum Tomfilm
Munchen: Kindler Verlag, 1956

Freĭlikh, Semen I.
Dramaturgie des Films
Berlin: Henschelverlag, 1964

Fuzelier, Étienne
Cinéma et Littérature
Paris: Éditions du Cerf, 1964

Gambetti, Giacomo
Comé si Guarda un Film; Cinema: Coscienza di un Fenomeno
Imola: P. Galeati, 1958

Georges, Paul
ABC du Cinéma: Lexique
Paris: Bloud and Gay, 1961

Gianeri, Enrico
Storia del Cartone Animato
Milano: Editrice Omnia, 1960

Glorius, Franz
Film, Jugend, Kirche
München: J. Pfeiffer, 1960

Gomes, Paulo E. S.
Jean Vigo
Paris: Éditions du Seuil, 1957

Grau, Jorge
El Actor y el Cine
Madrid: Ediciones Rialp, 1962

Guerrasio, Guido
Il Cinema, la Carne, e il Diavolo
Milano: Museo del Cinema, 1949

Hacquard, Georges
La Musique et le Cinéma
Paris: Presses Universitaires de France, 1959

Haro, Guillermo M.
La Dramaturgia Cinematográfica
Buenos Aires: Centro de Estudios Cinematográficos, 1957

Hovald, Patrice G.
Le Neo-realism Italien et ses Createurs
Paris: Éditions du Cerf, 1959

Idestam-Almquist, Bengt
Polsk Film Och den Nya Ryska Vägen
Stockholm: Wahlström and Widstrand, 1962

Idestam-Almquist, Bengt
Rysk Film: en Konstart Blir Till
Stockholm: Walström and Widstrand, 1962

L'information à travers le Monde. Presse, Radio, Télévision, Film
Paris: UNESCO, 1966

Jacchia, Paolo
Cinema Sovietico
Roma: Macchia, 1950

Jaulmes, Ph.
Cinéma, Temps et Espace; Introduction au Panrama: Procédé de Cinéma Total
Montpellier, 1963

Jeanne, René
Cinéma 1900
Paris: Flammarion, 1965

Jeanne, René and Charles Ford
Abel Gance
Paris: Éditions Seghers, 1963

Jeanne, René and Charles Ford
Le Cinéma et la Presse 1895-1960
Paris: A. Colin, 1961

Jeanne, René and Charles Ford
Histoire Encyclopédique du Cinéma
Paris: R. Laffont, 1947-62

Jeanne, René and Charles Ford
Les Vedettes de l'Écran
Paris: Presses Universitaires de France, 1964

Jeanne, René and Charles Ford
Victor Sjöström
Paris: Éditions Universitaires, 1963

Jewsiewicki, Władysław
Dějiny Polského Filmu
Preklad: Karešová, 1958

Jewsiewicki, Władysław
Kronika Kinematografi Światowej, 1895-1964
Warszawa: Wydawn, 1967

Jungersen, Frederik G.
Disney
København, Det Danske Filmmuseum, 1968

Kiehl, Jean
Les Ennemis du Théâtre: Essai sur les Rapports du Théâtre avec le Cinéma et la Littérature, 1918-1939
Nauchâtel: La Baconnière, 1951

Knietzsch, Horst
Film Gestern und Heute
Leipzig: Urania-Verlag, 1963

Knobel, Bruno
Wie ein Film Entsteht
Bern: Hallwag, 1955

Kyrou, Adonis
Amour, Érotisme et Cinéma
Paris: Le Terrain Vague, 1957

Kyrou, Adonis
Le Surrealisme au Cinéma
Paris: Arcanes, 1953

Lacalamita, Michele
Cinema e Narrativa
Roma: Bianco e Nero, 1959

Lacalamita, Michele and F. Di Gammatteo (eds.)
Filmlexicon Degli Autori e Delle Opere (7 vols.)
N.Y.: Benjamin Blom, 1968

Laclos, Michael
Le Fantastique au Cinéma
Paris: Jean-Jacques Pauvert, 1958

Laffay, Albert
Logique du Cinéma: Création et Spectacle
Paris: Masson, 1964

Lechesne, G.
La Salle de Cinéma Moderne
Paris: Nouvelles Éditions Film et Technique, 1955

Leirens, Jean
Le Cinéma et la Crise de Notre Temps
Paris: Éditions du Cerf, 1960

Leirens, Jean
Le Cinéma et le Temps
Paris: Éditions du Cerf, 1954

Lemaitres, Henri
Beaux-arts et Cinéma
Paris: Éditions du Cerf, 1956

Leon, Carlos A.
La Muerte en Hollywood, Ensayos
Caracas: Avila Gráfica, 1950

Leprohon, Pierre
Charles Chaplin
Paris: Nouvelles Éditions Debresse, 1957

Leprohon, Pierre
Chasseurs d'Images
Paris: A. Bonne, 1960

Leprohon, Pierre
Histoire du Cinéma
Paris: Éditions du Cerf, 1961

Leprohon, Pierre
Jean Epstein
Paris: Editions Seghers, 1964

Leprohon, Pierre
Les Mille et un Métiers du Cinéma
Paris: J. Melot, 1947

Leprohon, Pierre
Présences Contemporaines: Cinéma
Paris: Nouvelles Éditions Debresse, 1957

Lherminier, Pierre (ed.)
L'Art du Cinéma
Paris: Éditions Seghers, 1960

Lizzani, Carle
Le Cinema Italien
Firenze: Parenti, 1953

Lods, Jean
La Formation Professionnelle des Techniciens du Film
Paris: UNESCO, 1951

Lo Duca, Giuseppe
L'Érotisme au Cinéma
Paris: Jean-Jacques Pauvert, 1957-1962

Lo Duca, Giuseppe
Technique du Cinéma
Paris: Presses Universitaires de France, 1963

López Clemente, José
Cine Documental Español
Madrid: Ediciones Rialp, 1960

Lukács, György
Wider den Missverstandenen Realismus
Hamburg: Claassen, 1958

Lunders, Leo
L'attitude Actuelle des Jeunes devant le Cinéma
Bruxelles: Éditions du CEP, 1963

Malraux, André
Esquisse d'une Psychologie du Cinéma
Paris: Gallimard, 1946

Martin, Marcel
Le Estética de la Expresión Cinematográfica
Madrid: Ediciones Rialp, 1958

Martin, Marcel
Le Langage Cinématographique
Paris: Éditions du Cerf, 1955

Masetti, Enzo (comp.)
La Musica nel Film
Roma: Bianco e Nero Editore, 1950

Matoušek, František
Ruský ve Filmu
Praha: Československé Filmové Nakladatelství, 1946

Mauriac, Claude
L'amour du Cinéma
Paris: A. Michel, 1954

Mauriac, Claude
Petite Littérature du Cinéma
Paris: Éditions du Cerf, 1957

Les Méthodes d'Encouragement
à la Production et à la
Distribution des Films de
Court Métrage Destinés à une
Exploitation Commerciale
Paris: UNESCO, 1962

Michel, Manuel
El Cine y el Hombre
   Contemporáneo
Xalapa: Universidad
   Veracruzana, 1962

Miquel, Robert
Technique Moderne du Cinema
   Sonore
Paris: Société des Éditions
   Radio, 1955

Mitry, Jean
Charlot et la "Fabulation"
   Chaplinesque
Paris: Éditions Universitaires,
   1957

Mitry, Jean
Dictionnaire du Cinéma
Paris: Librairie Larousse, 1964

Mitry, Jean
Esthétique et Psychologie du
   Cinéma
   Vol. 1: Les Structures
   Vol. 2: Les Formes
Paris: Éditions Universitaires,
   1963, 1965

Mitry, Jean
Filmographie Universelle
Paris: Institut des Hautes Études
   Cinématographiques, 1963

Mitry, Jean
Griffith
Paris: Anthologie du Cinéma,
   1965

Mitry, Jean
Histoire du Cinéma: Art et
   Industrie, 1895-1914
Port Washington, N.Y.: Paris
   Pubs., 1967

Mitry, Jean
Ince
Paris: Imp. Spéciale de
   l'Anthologie du Cinéma, 1965

Mitry, Jean
John Ford
Paris Éditions Universitaires,
   1964

Mitry, Jean
René Clair
Paris: Éditions Universitaires,
   1960

Mitry, Jean
S. M. Eisenstein
Paris: Éditions Universitaires,
   1962

Morin, Edgar
Le Cinéma, ou l'Homme
   Imaginaire, Essai,
   d'Anthropologie Sociologique
Paris: Éditions de Minuit, 1956

Morin, Edgar
Les Stars
Paris: Éditions du Seuil, 1957

Moullet, Luc
Fritz Lang
Paris: Seghers, 1963

Mourlet, Michel
Cecil B. DeMille
Paris: Seghers, 1968

Naudín, Anna M.
Cine y Teatro
Barcelona: Editorial R. Sopena, 1965

Neergaard, Ebbe
Bog om Dreyer
København: Dansk Videnskabs Forlag, 1963

Nowak-Zaorska, Irena
Polski Film Oświatowy w Okresie Międzywojennym
Wrocław: Zakład Narodowy im. Ossolińskich, 1969

Paolella, Roberto
Storia del Cinema Muto
Napoli: Giannini, 1956

Pereira, José (ed.)
Teatro e Cinema
São Paulo: Exposição do Livro Editôra, 1961

Poncet, Marie T.
Dessin Animé, Art Mondial
Paris: Le Cercle du Livre, 1956

Prédal, René
Alain Resnais
Paris: Lettres Modernes, 1968

Premier Catalogue Sélectif International de Films Ethnographiques sue l'Afrique Noire
Paris: UNESCO, 1967

Prolo, Maria A.
Storia del Cinema Muto Italiano
Milano: Poligono, 1951

Proteau, Donald and Gérard Beaudet
Introduction au Cinéma
Montréal: Centre de Psychologie et de Pédagogie, 1966

Quéval, Jean
Marcel Carné
Paris: Cerf, 1952

Ragghianti, Carlo L.
Cinema, Arte Figurativa
Torino: G. Einaudi, 1952

Répertoire Mondial du Cinéma. Institutions S'intéressant aux Films Éducatifs, Scienfitiques et Culturels
Paris: UNESCO, 1962

Rieupeyrout, Jean L.
Le Western; ou, le Cinéma Américain par Excellence
Paris: Éditions du Cerf, 1953

Ritter, Claus
Seid nett Zueinander
Berlin: Henschelverlag, 1966

Roger, Jos
Grammaire du Cinéma
Bruxelles: Éditions Universitaires, 1954

Roger, Jos
Naissance d'un Film
Paris: Éditions Universitaires, 1956

Rognoni, Luigi
Cinema Muto, dalle Origine al
    1930
Roma: Bianco e Nero, 1952

Rohmer, Eric and Claude Chabrol
Hitchcock
Paris: Éditions Universitaires,
    1957

Rondi, Brunello
Il Neorealismo Italiano
Parma: Guanda, 1956

Rouch, Jean and Edgar Morin
Chronique d'un Été
Paris: Interspectacles, 1962

Sadoul, Georges
Le Cinéma Français (1890-1962)
Paris: Flammarion, 1962

Sadoul, Georges
Conquête du Cinéma
Paris: Gedalqe, 1960

Sadoul, Georges
Historie du Cinéma Mondial des
    Origines à Nos Jours
Paris: Flammarion, 1961 (6th
    ed.)

Sadoul, Georges
Les Merveilles de Cinéma
Paris: Les Éditeurs Français
    Réunis, 1957

Sadoul, Georges
Vie de Charlot: Charles Spencer
    Chaplin, ses Films et son
    Temps
Paris: Éditeurs Français Réunis,
    1957

Salachas, Gilbert
Federico Fellini
Paris: Éditions Seghers, 1963

Sarraute, Raymond and Michel
    Forline
Droit de la Cinématographie
Paris: Libraririe du Journal des
    Notaires et des Avocats, 1955

Sémolué, Jean
Bresson
Paris: Éditions Universitaires,
    1960

Sémolué, Jean
Dreyer
Paris: Éditions Universitaires,
    1962

Siclier, Jacques
La Femme dans le Cinéma
    Français
Paris: Éditions du Cerf, 1957

Siclier, Jacques
Ingmar Bergman
Paris: Éditions Universitaires,
    1960

Siclier, Jacques
Le Mythe de la Femme dans le
    Cinéma Américain: de "La
    Divine" à Blanche Dubois
Paris: Éditions du Cerf, 1956

Siclier, Jacques
Nouvelle Vaque?
Paris: Éditions du Cerf, 1961

Siclier, Jacques and Andre S.
    Labarthe
Images de la Science-Fiction
Paris: Éditions du Cerf, 1958

Silva, Francisco de Oliveira e
D. Quixote e Carlito
Rio de Janeiro: Editora Aurora, 1959

Slijeptević, Bosa
Jogoslovenski Film u Inostranim Filmskim Časopisima. Bibliografija 1947-1966
Beograd: Institut za Film, 1968

Souriau, Étienne (ed.)
L'Univers Filmique
Paris: Flammarion, 1953

Toeplitz, Jerzy
Film i Telewizja w USA: Ozień Dzisiejszy i Perspektywy
Warszawa: Wydawn, 1963

Traub, Hans and Hans W. Lavies
Das Deutsche Filmschrifttum: Cine Bibliographie der Bücher und Zeitschriften über das Filmwesen
Leipzig: Karl W. Hiersemann, 1940

Vaccaro, María R. (ed.)
Los Maestros de Antes, Hoy: Chaplin, Renoir, Clair, John Ford
Buenos Aires: Flashback, 1960

Vallet, Antoine
Les Genres du Cinéma
Paris: Legel, 1958

Vanto, Giovanni and Massimo Mida
Cinema e Resistenza
Firenze: Luciano Landi, 1959

Verdone, Mario
Historia del Cine
Madrid: Xáfaro, 1954

Verdone, Mario
Roberto Rossellini
Paris: Seghers, 1963

Vieyra, Paulin S.
Le Cinéma et l'Afrique
Paris: Présence Africaine, 1969

Villegas Lopéz, Manuel
Arte, Cine y Sociedad
Madrid: Taurus, 1959

Visconti, Luchino
La Caduta degli Dei
Bologna: Cappelli, 1969

Viviani, Almiro
Intorducão ao Cinema Brasileiro
Rio de Janeiro: Instituto Nacional do Livro, 1959

Waldekranz, Rune
Amerikansk Film
Stockholm: Wahlström and Widstrand, 1954

Waldekranz, Rune
Le Cinéma en Suède
Stockholm: Institut Suédois, 1953

Winkler, Gerd
Handbuch Film und Jugend
München: Juventa-Verlag, 1956

Zaccaria Soprani, Camilo
El Libro de los Artistas; Teoría y Práctica Cinematográfica: Televisión
Rosario: Editorial Soprani, 1948